From Pain to Purpose

From Pain to Purpose

A Young Woman's Journey from a Communist Prison to an American Pulpit

Luminitza C. Nichols

RESOURCE *Publications* • Eugene, Oregon

FROM PAIN TO PURPOSE
A Young Woman's Journey from a Communist Prison to an American Pulpit

Copyright © 2022 Luminitza C. Nichols. All rights reserved. Except for brief quotations in critical publications or reviews, no part of this book may be reproduced in any manner without prior written permission from the publisher. Write: Permissions, Wipf and Stock Publishers, 199 W. 8th Ave., Suite 3, Eugene, OR 97401.

Resource Publications
An Imprint of Wipf and Stock Publishers
199 W. 8th Ave., Suite 3
Eugene, OR 97401

www.wipfandstock.com

PAPERBACK ISBN: 978-1-6667-4860-4
HARDCOVER ISBN: 978-1-6667-4861-1
EBOOK ISBN: 978-1-6667-4862-8

10/03/22

Scripture quotations marked (NIV) are taken from the Holy Bible, New International Version®, NIV®. Copyright © 1973, 1978, 1984, 2011 by Biblica, Inc.™ Used by permission of Zondervan. All rights reserved worldwide. www.zondervan.com The "NIV" and "New International Version" are trademarks registered in the United States Patent and Trademark Office by Biblica, Inc.™

Scripture quotations marked (KJV) are taken from The Authorized (King James) Version. Rights in the Authorized Version in the United Kingdom are vested in the Crown. Reproduced by permission of the Crown's patentee, Cambridge University Press

Scripture quotations marked (NKJV) are taken from the Holy Bible, New King James Version®. Copyright © 1982 by Thomas Nelson. Used by permission. All rights reserved.

This book is a memoir. It reflects the author's present recollections of experiences over time. Some names and characteristics have been changed, some events have been compressed, and some dialogue has been recreated.

To Măicuța,
who kept her faith to the end

Contents

Acknowledgments | ix
Introduction | xi

1. Keep It to the End | 1
2. No Room for Gray | 8
3. The Call | 18
4. Faith in the Trenches | 30
5. Dress Rehearsal | 42
6. Truth Sends to Prison | 50
7. Who Is Christian Here? | 60
8. Doors No One Can Shut | 67
9. Windows in the Heavens | 77
10. No "Cats" in America | 87
11. Prison without Walls | 96
12. The Way Out | 110
13. "Do You Love Me?" | 121
14. What Locusts Have Eaten | 129
15. "Feed My Sheep" | 139

Acknowledgments

WRITING A BOOK IS never a solitary endeavor. It takes a "village" and thousands of moving parts to birth forth what you are now holding in your hands. So, here are some of the "villagers" to whom I am especially grateful for making this project happen: my husband, Eric, whose support and patience have been of biblical proportions through the entire writing process. Thank you, love, for believing I could do this. I am grateful to our daughters, Ana and Teodora, who reminded me that I was an author, even when I didn't feel like one. Thank you, ladies, for allowing me to be a working mom and never complaining when dinner was simple. And with the risk of sounding cliché, I am grateful to my Lord Jesus Christ, the "Chief Villager," who allowed my life to be so colorful that people would want to read about it.

Introduction

THE SICKLE-SHAPED LEAVES CRUSHED like shattered glass under my hammer-heel boots. It was 1979 in Communist Romania. The first day of school was always exciting because, on that day, we received our textbooks for the year. I leafed through one book and felt an urge to pick up a pen and draw. The picture on the first page beckoned for a remake. It was a well-known portrait of our dictator. So, I pressed the pen and drew a mustache, glasses, and horns on his head.

A few days later, my father discovered my masterpiece. Never in my life had I seen him so angry and afraid all at once. He shouted something about going to *pârnaie*, which was slang for the big house, the infamous prison in our city. My tiny body shook. I knew that writing in a schoolbook was not a capital offense, so it must have been my irreverent drawing on the face of the president. I tried to erase it to no avail. Ripping the page had even worse consequences. What was I supposed to do now?

From as early as preschool, I was taught to pay homage to the president with a semblance of fun that made it seem inconsequential that I, with others my age, was being conditioned to become a good little communist.

Introduction

But that day, the big question in my nine-year-old mind was: Why did my father fear this man? Was I, too, supposed to fear him?

I had yet to find my answers.

Chapter 1

Keep It to the End

ALL HUMANS HAVE AT least one thing in common. We all come from someplace on the map we call home. Romania happened to be mine. Timișoara, to be exact. A city known for its roses, eclectic culture, and beautiful girls. The only city in that blessed land where hope still flickered in communism before it, too, succumbed to the mournful screech of the dirge. Timișoara was my city, my home, and my little corner of heaven during my brief growing-up years.

My parents came from different villages, one from the north and the other from the south, and met in the middle, in the big city of Timișoara. My mother grew up Protestant, and my father was Orthodox. But since neither observed their family's faith traditions, my sister and I were christened according to cultural expectations in the Eastern Orthodox Church. If family squabbles ever arose over religious affiliation, the christening of children, usually, settled the matter. But life is rarely predictable.

I was six years old when my mother became a "Repenter"—a pejorative term used in our country to mock Protestants. Over the years, this name became the most precious and the most despised

1

From Pain to Purpose

human label in Romania. My father, Iosif, proudly named after the Soviet dictator Ioseb Stalin, was among those who despised it. He gave my mother one week to change her mind or leave us. Raising two daughters without a mother was infinitely less painful than being married to a Repenter. The shame was simply too great to bear. But that week, my father fell ill, my mother nursed him to health, and that ended his persecution.

When it came to parenting, my parents agreed on at least one thing: Children should roam hills and climb trees, not be cooped up in city block apartments. So, every summer, we packed our family car, and my parents took my sister and me to relatives living in different villages. By the time I was ten, I could milk cows, rake hay, and switch between regional accents so quickly that I could fool a local.

When my parents visited us, usually for my birthday in August, my mother took my sister and me, and we climbed several hills to the only Protestant church in that county. There, we sang songs, and my mother shared words of encouragement with a handful of Repenters.

My mother had a powerful gift of evangelism, and many came to faith because of her. In our house, no room was off limits for worship. She knelt anywhere to pray and sang "lustily" to the Lord. My mother was the first Spirit-filled Christian I ever knew. Her love for the Lord moved me as a child.

Five years later, however, every visible sign of my mother's faith had disappeared. She had made some unwise choices and could not see a way out, much less receive forgiveness. My mother stopped going to church, and the joy of salvation faded from her face.

Five years older myself, I had almost forgotten what I had learned from my mother. Church held little appeal while the world lured me farther away with its luscious fruit. Then one day, a new classmate arrived. Her name was Nuți, and when her older sister came to pick her up from school, something about her seemed strikingly familiar. Nuți's sister had that classic look of a Repenter, with long hair, no makeup, no jewelry, and a countenance all too similar to what I had once seen of my mother.

The following day I asked Nuți if she and her family were Repenters. Protestants were ill-treated in our country, so she avoided an answer and responded instead with a question:

"Is this what you ask every new student that comes to this school?"

I assured her that she had nothing to fear since my mother used to be a Repenter and that I had gone to church with my mother when I was little. Nuți admitted that everyone in her family was a Repenter, but she had not yet committed.

Such could have been the end of our conversation until, one day, Nuți overheard me saying to another classmate that I wanted to learn to play the guitar but that my parents wouldn't pay for lessons. Not wasting a moment, Nuți interrupted:

"I know someone who could teach you to play guitar for free if you are interested."

Her offer piqued my interest, especially since I wouldn't have to ask my parents for money.

When the day of my first guitar lesson arrived, Nuți picked me up from home and I was gleaming with excitement. We walked briskly against the winter wind for almost an hour. Then, Nuți stopped, looked both ways, and entered a house tucked behind a building that stored horse-drawn funerary carriages. I followed her inside.

From the street, the building resembled an ordinary house, but inside, the dividing walls between rooms had been removed, and at least one hundred chairs were neatly lined, facing a wooden platform. The walls were mostly bare, except for a few black plaques engraved with Bible verses and the map of the Holy Land covering most of the water stains on the back wall.

"This is not somebody's house," I thought to myself in a sudden panic. "This is an illegal, underground church!"

I looked around the room for the exit when a young man appeared at the door and greeted us with a big smile and a hearty handshake:

From Pain to Purpose

"Hi, my name is Emanuel. Please come in."

He led us into a room where a group of young people close to my age, all holding guitars, sat in a semicircle. Before I could get my bearings, Emanuel placed a guitar in my lap, and I was on my way to learning my first song.

When the lesson ended, he told us to take the guitars home to practice our chords before the next class. I gazed at Nuți as if to say, "They teach you for free *and* let you take the guitar home?" Nuți didn't seem surprised.

On our way home, I didn't do my usual rambling. I clumsily carried the guitar, trying not to bang it against the walls fencing the narrow streets. Nuți and I had entirely different personalities, which was probably the reason we made such good friends. She was quiet and reflective, and I was insufferably talkative. But that evening, one could only hear our footsteps pounding the ground in the same cadence.

In my bedroom that night, I practiced the song Emanuel taught us, "We Are One in the Spirit, We Are One in the Lord." It had two basic chords on the guitar, and I was determined to learn them.

Every week, Nuți and I walked to the little house church for guitar lessons, and every week we learned new Christian songs. In my eagerness to play the guitar, I had forgotten my initial apprehension about the church.

My parents paid no attention to me, neither when I hummed hymns throughout the house nor when I practiced my guitar chords. Only occasionally, when my father couldn't take my repetitive strumming anymore, he would yell from the other room for me to stop. In a short time, I could play several songs, and accompany by ear melodies I had never learned. But there was something else that kept me going to guitar lessons week after week.

In many respects, those young Christians and I were pretty similar. We were all children of the 1980s who shared the same love for the decade's iconic music and fashion. Yet, there was something about them that I could not figure out.

Keep It to the End

The abject misery inflicted by communism was evident all around us. Food was rationed. Electricity, heat, and warm water were cut off to only a few hours a day. Any words interpreted as criticism of the government could land any one of us in jail, which added another layer of anxiety to an already tormented people. Yet, despite it all, my Christian friends looked as if they lived in an entirely different world than everyone else. They seemed to possess an intrinsic peace that lifted them above the worst of circumstances. They sang and smiled for no apparent reason, with a joy not forced but coming from deep inside. How was that possible? Didn't they know that they were supposed to be miserable like the rest of us?

One Tuesday morning at school, Nuți appeared eager to tell me something. Beaming from ear to ear, she whispered, "Yesterday, I became a Repenter. A pastor is visiting from out of town, and he is here only until tomorrow. Will you come to church with me to hear him speak?"

I don't know why, but I felt a visceral reaction against going to a church service. I had already determined that I would not become a Christian. And while I appreciated the free guitar lessons, my eyes were riveted upon the sight of some young men in my neighborhood, and I knew I couldn't be a Repenter and go out with those cute unbelievers at the same time. When she insisted, I snapped:

"Fine, I'll come, but I won't become a Repenter!"

"You don't have to. Just come and hear him speak," Nuți said.

The next evening when we arrived at church, the courtyard was packed. Inside the building, there was barely room to stand. The condensation on the walls and windows dripped like long strips of rain inside a cave, and the air felt stuffy, but no one seemed to care. People parted the way to let us through, and several stood to offer us their chairs. Nuți pointed forward to her two sisters who saved us seats beside them.

From Pain to Purpose

Gazing around the room, I recognized some of the young people who learned guitar with me. They looked pleased to see us. Then, for an entire hour, we all stood while nearly everybody prayed aloud, first the men and then the women. And at last, we sat down to sing.

A few minutes later, a man in his early forties stepped behind the wooden pulpit and opened a tattered Bible almost too small for his large hands. His name was Petrică Dugulescu—a man, I later learned, hunted by the secret police for his growing influence among university students. As he read from the tattered book, his voice reached a crescendo that commanded attention. He spoke about a man named Peter, and Jesus who called Peter to come to him walking on water. One could hear a pin drop.

With my mouth slightly opened, my eyes stayed fixed upon the preacher until suddenly, he turned, pointed in my direction, and said, "Just like Peter, Jesus is calling you tonight to come to him."

My body sunk into the chair. I didn't expect to be singled out like that in a crowd, nor did I expect the flood of emotions that engulfed me at that moment. It was a combination of shortness of breath mixed with a compelling urgency to respond outwardly. I looked at Nuți, but she and her two sisters had their eyes closed. When Pastor Petrică asked a second time, who would come to Jesus just as Peter came, a power beyond my control shot my right arm straight up into the air. A few moments later, I stood at the front of the church, as Pastor Petrică prayed for me.

It was November and probably dreary outside, I don't recall. But what I remember is that my feet hardly touched the ground the entire way home. My heart felt too small to contain the heavenly presence I suddenly carried, and I thought I could burst if I didn't soon tell someone the news.

After I said goodbye to Nuți and her sisters, I floated up the stairs to our apartment where everyone was asleep. Holding my breath, I tiptoed past my parents' bedroom. I didn't want to wake

Keep It to the End

them, nor did I want to tell them what happened at church. But I knew that my grandmother wouldn't mind if I awoke her.

Măicuța, as we called her, was my mother's mother. Every winter, she stayed with us in the city until planting season in the spring. She, her husband, and her own mother had been among the first Protestants in the village of Râpa in the late 1920s. There, they started the first Baptist church, which remains strong to this day.

In my grandmother's room, I dropped to my knees next to her bed. I intended to whisper, but the words came out in a whistle-like sound.

"Măicuța, I surrendered to the Lord tonight!"

Pulling herself up, she shielded her eyes from the ceiling light. Then, in her thick village accent, she said something I would only later come to fully understand:

"*Numa' și țâi pân' la capăt*," she whispered.

I pondered her words for a moment before I floated out of her room and into my bedroom.

"Just keep it until the end? Is that it?" I said to myself.

I knew Măicuța was happy for me, but she certainly didn't show it. Her words seemed somber, almost foreboding.

My grandmother became a Repenter when she was twenty-five years old. She lived through two world wars, buried three of her children, and suffered the death of both her mother and husband in the same year, which left her nearly destitute. For almost eighty years, Măicuța knew little ease and much about keeping the faith until the end. But now, in communism, she could only imagine the price I would have to pay for that night's decision.

Chapter 2

No Room for Gray

VIOLENCE AGAINST PROTESTANT CHRISTIANS mounted. Pastors and church leaders underwent brutal interrogations and were pressured to become informants for the secret police. Most underground churches were penalized with heavy fines if discovered or were permanently shut down. Owning a Bible was considered illegal, similar to drugs and guns. And all Christian literature, if found, was confiscated and destroyed. Life in Romania was becoming unbearable.

I just started the eighth grade, and at the end of the school year, I planned to compete for a place in the nursing high school. All secondary schools in Romania were vocational schools that guaranteed jobs in that field upon graduation, so the competition was fierce for the best high schools in the city, nursing being one of them.

Despite the difficulty of the exam, I yearned to learn more about my new faith. I prayed and read my Bible for hours each day and impatiently waited for my forthcoming baptism the following March. In the meantime, I met weekly with the church deacons for catechism. These were preparatory lessons that taught more than the basics of Christianity. They focused on persecution and the cost of following Christ.

"This faith in Jesus is not something you add to your regular life," one deacon said during our first catechism lesson. "Your faith is your life, and it may cost you your life. Do you still want it?"

Then, another deacon added: "You may go to prison for your faith. You may lose your job, your relationships, and your reputation if you become a Repenter. Do you still want it?" As they spoke, these were not rhetorical questions. All baptismal candidates had to consider them carefully and then one by one we had to answer a confident, "Yes."

After catechism, the last step before baptism was to share with the whole church how I accepted Christ, and then the church would discern together if I was ready to be baptized. Knowing that my parents would never agree to it, I kept my baptism a secret. I wrote the testimony I intended to give before the church on a piece of paper and carried it to school with me so my parents wouldn't find it.

Every day I rehearsed my testimony and then put it back into a hidden pocket inside my bookbag. But one day, when I returned from recess, I had a sick feeling that the paper was gone. I ran to my seat to check. The paper had disappeared. Somebody ransacked my bag and took only that paper but nothing else. This was absurd since no one knew about it.

The following class was biology. The professor, a physician in town, liked me because I planned to compete for the nursing high school. Suddenly, a knock interrupted the lecture. Instantly I knew that it had something to do with me. A student entered the classroom and announced: "Cristescu Luminița is asked to go to the principal's office."

The somber inflection in his voice gave away that the matter was grave. The professor glanced suspiciously at me, and I could hear my classmates whisper what they thought I might have done. Only bad students were called into the principal's office, especially in the middle of a lecture.

From Pain to Purpose

I walked the long corridor, touching the walls, trying to hide from the student escorting me that I was shaking. I had never done anything illegal before. What was I going to say?

Inside the principal's office, the dictator's portrait loomed large on the main wall facing the door—an inescapable reminder that everyone was being watched. The principal sat lounging in a chilling posture behind a conference table, and I stopped in front of him, head down, as expected of a student in trouble.

He was smoking, intentionally letting the ashes miss the ashtray and fall onto a sheet of paper, all the while watching me as he flicked his cigarette. I glanced down and recognized my handwriting. His eyes bore into me. There was no point in him telling me what he thought of my paper.

I prayed in my mind that whatever he might do to me would be over quickly, and my parents would never find out. But to my surprise, he asked what high school I had in mind to compete for at the close of the school year. He seemed passive. Not at all how I expected a principal to be. Then, after a brief pause, he glanced at my paper and spoke dismissively:

"About this, all I can tell you is that you will regret it. You will have no life, and it will bring you only hardships. You are young, so take my advice. Change your mind now."

I couldn't believe my ears. No threats. No slapping. Only advice. I looked at the principal, and the words popped out of my mouth.

"Thank you, but I will not change my mind."

He motioned me to the door.

On my way out, I couldn't believe what had just happened. I left the classroom trembling with fear and returned entirely in control.

No one asked what happened in the principal's office, not even Nuți, and I never mentioned it to anyone at church. But in my heart, I knew that a foundation was laid that day, upon which I was ready to build.

No Room for Gray

A week before my baptism, I didn't have a white dress and didn't know where to find one. Churches did not keep baptismal robes on hand, and there was no option to buy one from the store. Women usually sewed their baptismal dress, borrowed one, or had someone make it for them. I knew no one who could help me.

Moreover, the deacons were still undecided as to whether to approve me for baptism. They believed that not having parents who supported my decision would make it difficult for me to remain faithful until the end. They were concerned that family, school, and government opposition would simply be too much for a teenager to bear.

The Friday before Sunday's baptismal service I was still waiting to hear from the deacons about their decision. Around seven o'clock in the evening, the phone rang. From the other end of the line, Nuți shouted:

"They are letting you get baptized! A deacon just called."

I could barely keep from screaming and giving myself away. I mentioned to Nuți that I didn't have a white dress for baptism, hoping that she could help me. But she knew of no one my size or who could sew or loan me a dress at the last minute. The following morning the phone rang.

"Sure, you can come by today," my mother said to the person on the other end of the line.

An hour later, a young woman appeared at the door and handed me a bag.

"It's your mother's baptismal dress. I borrowed it three years ago when I got baptized. I'm sorry it took me so long to return it."

I stared at her dumbfounded. I grabbed the bag and ran inside. "Could it be that this God in whom I'm putting my trust even cares about a dress?" I wondered. But there was no time to waste. Somehow, I needed to take the dress to Nuți's apartment without anyone noticing.

My mother opened the bag and said glibly, "Yeah, I was pretty skinny back then," and tossed the dress onto the bed. I waited until she was busy with dinner and checked the dress next to my body for size. "It'll have to do," I said to myself.

"Lumi! Can you run to the store? We need bread. Take five Lei[1] from my purse," my mother shouted from the kitchen.

"Perfect," I thought. I hid the dress inside my coat and ran as fast as I could to Nuți's apartment.

It had been seven years since my mother made her covenant with Christ in baptism, and now it meant so little to her. But to be baptized in my mother's dress was a sure sign that God was not finished with our family.

I must have said to my mother that Nuți was getting baptized that Sunday, because the following day, as I was preparing myself for church, my mother called me into her bedroom.

"I hope you are not getting baptized today!" my mother said.

I hesitated.

"Aren't baptisms usually held during the evening service? I'm not planning on going tonight," I said, being intentionally evasive. My mother seemed satisfied with my answer because she went back to sleep.

Many churches held baptismal services on Sunday evenings, and my mother knew this. But our church, for some reason, baptized on Sunday mornings. Nuți's mother had ironed my dress and brought it to church. I wore a thick turtleneck underneath, and the dress fit perfectly.

Baptisms were the grandest of all celebrations. But in communism, Protestant baptisms were also risky. They represented an act of defiance against everything an atheist regime engendered. Every new believer who publicly professed faith in Jesus Christ faced imminent persecution and suffering.

That morning, the church was packed, and the service lasted over three hours. The entire time, I sat on the edge of my seat, watching every entrance into the sanctuary. I imagined that at any

1. Romanian currency.

No Room for Gray

moment, my father would appear in one of those doors and drag me out of the church by my hair.

But when I emerged from the water, drenched from head to toe, I knew one thing for sure, that no one could take this away from me, and I didn't care what awaited me on the other side of my baptism. The rest of the day I walked on clouds, and it was so hard to keep it all inside.

In the following weeks, the joy of my salvation translated into an outright enthusiasm to do everything I once dreaded. I washed the dishes. I cleaned the house. I took the trash out. All of this, and more, I did without being asked, and to my parents' utter dismay. At times, my mother's prolonged stares made me think that perhaps she suspected something. But she never confirmed my suspicions.

Nuți and I were inseparable. We spent our school recesses whispering about Jesus, and at my house, on sleepover nights, we memorized entire chapters from the Bible until the wee hours of the morning.

One day at school, Nuți handed me an envelope and told me to open it at home. Inside was a stack of black and white pictures of our baptism. In my room that night, I looked through the faded photographs for what must have been an hour, reliving each moment immortalized in them. Suddenly, the door of my bedroom flung open. There stood my mother with her finger pointing to the pictures.

"Don't tell me what those are! I will tell you! You got baptized, and those are your baptism pictures."

I froze. How did she know?

"Will you tell Tati?" I asked, trying not to show that I was scared.

She grabbed the pictures and thumbed through them like through a deck of cards.

"I won't tell your father. But he may find them if you leave them lying around. I'll take them to my brother's house."

From Pain to Purpose

I let out a sigh of relief.

A week later, I heard my parents arguing in the kitchen. My father was angry with my mother, and in the middle of their argument, I heard my mother say, "You think what I did was bad? What about Lumi? Did you know that she got baptized?"

I could not believe my ears. Their argument had nothing to do with me. She threw me under the bus to divert my father's wrath from her. She was now off the hook, but I could hear my father charging toward my room. I braced myself for the impact.

"What do you think you're doing?" He shouted, pointing his finger at me. "Do you think you can do whatever you want in this house? You made yourself the enemy of this family. That's all I'm going to tell you."

My back was still pressed against the wall when my father left the room. I loved my family. I was not their enemy. But in my heart, I could hear the words of Jesus: "For I have come to turn a man against his father, a daughter against her mother, and your enemies will be members of your own family."[2]

I don't know what I expected my father to do next, but I was not surprised when a few days later, his three siblings showed up at our door.

For a communist apartment, our kitchen was quite large and served also as a sitting room. The family often gathered there to talk, and children were never allowed to hear those conversations. But this time, my father ordered me into the kitchen. My mother pulled out the shot glasses and began to serve my father's homemade hard liquor. When my parents presented my "crime," everyone appeared concerned.

One of my aunts who came that day was also my godmother. Her role in the Orthodox tradition was to make sure that, as I grew, my relationship with God developed properly. Ironically, she seemed the most offended by my faith in God.

---

2. Matt 10:35–36 KJV.

No Room for Gray

"I baptized you into the true church. You didn't need another baptism," she shouted at me, while everyone agreed.

Orthodoxism was the dominant Christian religion in Romania and was tolerated by our socialist state. Orthodox leaders rarely suffered persecution, although some who had sought to bring renewal within the Orthodox Church had been persecuted.

Most Romanians were baptized into the Orthodox Church and called themselves Christians, but few lived according to the precepts of Christianity. For that reason, Protestants viewed the Orthodox faith as an apostate faith, while the Orthodox Church called Protestantism a Western religion and, therefore, not the true faith of the apostles. The main Protestant denominations became known as "sects," and anyone who converted to Protestantism could expect to be persecuted first by their Orthodox family members and most assuredly by the government.

Repenters were often expelled from universities or were forbidden to enroll altogether in higher education. It was the government's attempt to maintain the narrative that Protestants were anti-intellectual.

For the rest of the evening, this was my family's main argument. One after another, they implored me to wait until I was older and secured first a good career. They insisted that my decision to join the Protestants would destroy my professional and social future, not to mention the dishonor it brings upon the family. They asked me to renounce my faith right then and there.

As they were speaking, I was not allowed to sit, leave the room, or say anything in my defense. So, my mind drifted to the day I gave my life to Christ. How happy God's presence made me feel and how real it was! How can I give it up or pretend that it never happened?

"Brother, this is all your fault!" my uncle—a successful head of a company and outspoken atheist—zinged at my father. My father's eyebrows furrowed. My uncle then pointed to the Baptist calendar hanging on the wall above him.

From Pain to Purpose

"Your children are running this home. You are not the man of your house, or you would not allow such things plastered on your walls."

My father hesitated for a moment, then reached up and, with one fell swoop of his hand, ripped the calendar off the wall and threw it into the garbage. As I watched him, I felt a sudden sadness for my father. He looked like a little boy peer-pressured into doing something to please his older brother. For a moment, the room fell silent, only the sound of ripping paper lingered in my ears.

My mother rushed to refill everyone's glass with moonshine, and the more they drank, the louder they became. When they exhausted all their niceties, the room turned into a chaotic free-for-all. Talking over each other, they shouted profanities, blasphemed God, and mocked the Bible and everything I held dear. With every ounce of strength, I tried to hold back my tears, but the dam was breaking.

My father sat quietly, letting his siblings score their points, while my mother faithfully kept refilling their shot glasses. Tears dripped down my cheeks faster than I could wipe them. Would no one defend me?

I looked at my mother, knowing that she endured the same wrath from these very people seven years earlier, and for the same reason. But she didn't make eye contact. With a fake smile, she kept on mechanically refilling their glasses.

I reached for the door, but my father ordered me to stay until they were finished with me. Five adults surrounding like a pack of wolves a thirteen-year-old because she believed in God! How right the deacons were. My road was not going to be easy.

When I was finally allowed to leave the kitchen, I ran into my bedroom and threw myself on my knees next to my bed. I could no longer swallow my tears. I held my Bible to my chest and cried out, "Father, this is too hard! I don't know if I can endure to the end."

I opened the Bible, and the words on the page spoke almost audibly:

"Now get up and stand on your feet. I have appeared to you to appoint you as a servant and as a witness of what you have seen and will see of me. I will rescue you from your own people . . . to whom I am sending you to open their eyes and turn them from darkness to light, and from the power of Satan to God, so that they may receive forgiveness of sins and a place among those who are sanctified by faith in me."[3]

The commanding words of Scripture startled me, and I could do nothing but obey. I stood on my feet and instantly my tears dried and my heartache disappeared as if someone had removed it by hand. How can God's word do this with such ease?

Outside my room, I could hear my relatives leave. I lay on the bed still staring in awe at my Bible. I couldn't stop thinking about what had just happened: I went to my knees a battered girl and stood up as a confident young woman with a mission from God—to turn my family from darkness to light. As I drifted off to sleep, I knew that another brick was laid that day upon the foundation that was Christ.

---

3. Acts 26:16–18 KJV.

Chapter 3

The Call

I ENTERED THE NINTH grade disillusioned about my academic abilities. I had not passed the nursing high school entrance exam, and my parents and relatives didn't hesitate to point out that church was the primary factor that distracted me from my schoolwork. But, since I had failed the exam with a relatively high grade, I was eligible to register at a different high school in the city to continue my studies.

The first day at the new school was standard, as one would expect. But I started to learn that nothing was ever standard in communism when Christians were in a room—as if our very presence disturbed the atmosphere of the enemy. Around mid-morning, the classroom door opened, slamming into the opposing wall as the high school principal made his entrance.

"Who is a Repenter here?" he bellowed, without so much as saying hello.

The teacher stopped the lecture, and the students held their breath. I was taken aback by the suddenness of the question and hesitated for a second. But the principal was on a roll.

"I know that you, Repenters, are not allowed to lie, so stand up if you are a Baptist or Pentecostal," he shouted again.

The Call

I was seated in the front row, right in front of him, and when I stood, the eyes of thirty petrified students shifted in my direction. The principal wrote down my name and slammed the door behind him.

I sat in my chair, wondering what this would mean for the next four years of my life. That day, my name became "Repentich," a mockery of the word "Repenter." The name stuck, and my high school journey began.

In secondary school, each new ninth-grade class was assigned a teacher-mentor. These were parent-like figures or life coaches whose task was to guide us through the rough years of adolescence. I should not have been surprised when our class mentor turned out to be the most hard-core communist professor in all high school. Her weekly life coaching sessions consisted almost exclusively of Communist Party propaganda.

"Who in the twentieth century still believes that there is a God?" she often hollered, as if angry with this God she didn't believe existed. "Religion has no place in modern socialist society," she yelled, pounding her desk.

Then, she would summon me to stand in front of the room facing my classmates while she urged them to laugh at me for still believing in God. Some laughed. Most did not. But the pain was all the same.

Communist schools permitted corporal punishment, but instructors rarely applied it in high school unless they were bent upon a mission to use shaming as a teaching method. In this case, Protestant pupils were their easiest targets. They had no legal recourse, and no one dared to defend them.

In high school, students had to report to school on Christmas Day and Easter, and mandatory field trips were often scheduled on Sundays in an obvious attempt to prevent young people from going to church. I was the only one who never showed up for field trips or came to school on major Christian holidays.

From Pain to Purpose

But my defiance of communism made my teacher-mentor especially furious. She took it as a personal failure, and she must have complained about it to the rest of the faculty, because one day, in the middle of her lecture, the vice principal—a woman whose husband was a feared communist city official—stormed into our classroom and pointed directly at me to go into the hallway.

Before I closed the door behind me, she grabbed hold of my hair and dragged me the full length of the corridor. I could hear her gasp like a wounded animal. She slapped me with one hand and pulled my hair with the other.

In my four years at the school, she and I never had a single conversation. Nor was she ever my instructor or knew my name. I was among hundreds of students in that school, but she unleashed her fury on me with absolute precision. Then, she pulled a comb from her pocket and threw it on the floor.

"Pick it up and go fix your hair. You look disgraceful," she lambasted.

It was days before graduation.

While many cherish their high school memories, mine consisted mainly of ceremonial mockeries, beatings, and threats that my belief in God would hinder my graduation.

And yet, it was at home, not at school, where my faith took the hardest hits. My parents continued to view my Christian convictions as an affront to their authority—a dangerous sectarian indoctrination that jeopardized my success in life.

My father was a political activist, although he would never admit it. I still remember the day when he proudly told me that he became the president of the Communist Party at his workplace. Over the years, he had acquired multiple medals and awards for his contribution to the advancement of communism, and, by law, he was not permitted to have Repenters among his immediate family members if he sought to keep his position.

Often, he threatened to throw me out of the house and forbade me to go to church. But whenever he wasn't looking or was

The Call

simply too drunk to notice, I ran to church as fast as I could, not knowing what would happen when I came home. Several families in our church offered to take me in, if or when that was to happen.

My sister, Dorina, was the golden child. After hearing of my baptism, she wanted nothing to do with me. She joined forces with my father, and together they ridiculed me or ignored me in the house.

At school and at home I didn't belong, and I prayed every day that God would take me home. I was not depressed. On the contrary, I was filled with joy and faith, but I yearned to be with Jesus who loved me, rather than in a house where no one seemed to want me. But if God had a purpose for my life, as he said, I desperately needed him to make it clear.

One day I rummaged through a drawer in my parents' bedroom and found a booklet that belonged to my mother from the time when she went to church. The title intrigued me: *What It Means to Be a True Disciple*. I hid the booklet under my arm and locked myself in my room to read it. With every page I turned, my heart pounded faster. The book spoke of mission fields, martyrdom, and people who gave their lives to the cause of Christ. As I read, joy began to rise inside me like a swelling tide. "This is it! This is what I want to do with the rest of my life," I said to myself. More than anything in the world I wanted to be like those people in the book, fully sold out to Christ. That day, I wrote in my Bible: "Lord, make me a missionary and help me one day to die for my faith."

Although Christian literature was illegal in Romania, soon, another book fell into my hands. It was about Mary Slessor, the Scottish missionary to Africa. I have no recollection of who gave me the book or who translated it into Romanian. But as I read it, I fell in love with the African continent and prayed that the Lord someday would send me there as a missionary. I didn't know that what I was sensing was a call to the ministry. Every day after school, I spent hours on my knees praying and dreaming about mission fields. In my leisure time, I wrote sermons that I preached whispering in my room at night.

From Pain to Purpose

One day at church, I mentioned my sermon-writing habit to a girl in our youth group. She looked at me as if I was supposed to know something that everybody knew but me. When I was younger, I saw my mother ministering in village churches. I didn't know that preaching was not an authorized role for women. At church, I savored every word coming from the pastor's mouth, feeling as though I stood in the pulpit with him, finishing his sentences. Surely, I thought, other girls felt the same way.

At this time, someone told me that in America there were universities where one could study the Bible. I couldn't imagine a place in the world where people studied the Bible without threat or intrusion, and I wanted more than anything in the world to do that. I didn't know how it could come to pass. Communist authorities prohibited Romanians from leaving the country at will. But, with childlike faith, I prayed that someday God would open doors for me to study at a Bible school in America. In every human way, this was an impossibility!

I was fourteen when a young man entered my life. We were both from unbelieving families and needed mentors in the faith. It was not long before an old saint and a godly woman took us under their wings, and every week we met in their homes to learn how to keep our faith until the end.

At home, every time I had a chance, I shared the gospel with my father. I loved him so much that I couldn't fathom spending eternity without him. I fasted days in a row for his salvation and went so far as to ask God to let me die, just so my father would hear the gospel at my funeral and accept Christ. It was a crazy prayer, but I didn't know how else to intercede for him.

My father, on the other hand, remained unbending. Then one day, after dinner, he followed me into the hallway.

"Hey, isn't it true that you call God your father?" he asked.

I knew where he was going with the question.

"Yes," I replied, rushing toward my bedroom.

The Call

"Tell me then, who pays for your food, God or me? Who puts a roof over your head? Who buys your clothes, God, or me?"

He didn't wait for my answer.

"If God is your father, then I am your God," he thundered. He followed behind me, hammering home his point.

"Do you hear me? I am your God!"

I backed off.

"You are my earthly father. You are not God," I said.

My father's eyes bulged out.

"So long as you live in my house, I am your God. Do you hear me? Call me God!"

"No, I won't. You are not God."

"I . . . am . . . your . . . God!" he shouted.

And with the force of those words, my father's hand struck across my face, flinging my head violently to the side. Everything inside me screamed that I should run and lock myself in my room, when, suddenly, an inner voice, as clear as any human voice, stopped me in mid-movement.

"Turn the other cheek," the voice said.

I looked at my father and slowly turned my face. Without hesitating, he struck me again with the back of his hand.

"I am your God. Do you hear me?"

I looked into his eyes, tears dripping down my numb cheeks. My ears rang, and my jaw felt loose. I turned my face ten times before my father showed signs of slowing down. Suddenly, my sister bolted out of her bedroom shouting, "Slap me, too, because I believe what she believes!"

My father's mouth fell open. The look on Dorina's face left no doubt that she meant every word. My eyes shifted back and forth between my father and my sister. What will my father do? Will he slap her, too? Defeated, my father lowered his head and walked away.

My sister had been to church with me only a few times and had never made a public profession of faith. But, oh, how worth it were every tear I shed and every slap I endured to see my sister make her stand for Christ that day!

From Pain to Purpose

In my room, I sat motionless on the edge of the bed. I didn't know whether to cry for pain or cry for joy, when, in my spirit, I heard a familiar voice:

"Let me go after him!"

It was not the first time the Lord had said that to me after one of my father's tirades, and I always responded the same way. I fell to my knees and begged God to hold back his hand.

"Forgive him, Lord, he doesn't know what he's doing. Don't punish him for what he doesn't know." But this time, I could feel that God was angry with my father.

Early the following morning, I heard a commotion in the hallway outside my bedroom. I peeked through the door and saw my father. His face looked monstrous. His mouth was distorted, unable to close, and enormous bags of puss protruded from under his upper lip extending from one cheek to another. My sister ran trembling into my bedroom.

"Lumi, do you think God is punishing Tati for what he did to you yesterday?"

The thought had crossed my mind, but I didn't want to say it. "I don't know, Dori. I don't know."

In December that same year, our church announced that we would spend New Year's Eve in an all-night prayer and fellowship vigil. The women brought in delicious food, and we prayed, worshiped, and talked through the night.

The deacons created a game similar to drawing lots before the Lord. They wrote Bible verses on small pieces of paper they nestled inside empty pecan shells and then prayed over them to be "words in season" for those who drew them.

While the deacons handed out the verses, I began to pray. I needed the Lord to speak to me specifically about my future. If he truly called me to ministry, I needed to find his answer in one of those nutshells. I picked a verse from the bag and held it tightly in my hand as I continued to pray, "Lord, speak to me about my future."

The Call

I slowly opened the nutshell, and written on the tiny piece of paper was Daniel 12:3. I didn't know the verse, so I scrambled to find my Bible. The presence of the Lord felt like waves of joy bubbling inside me. Then, I read: "Those who are wise will shine like the brightness of the sky, and those who will teach many to walk in righteousness like the stars forever and ever."[1] For the next few moments, every sound around me became muffled, only those words echoed in my ears.

One after another, deacons, laypeople, and church leaders read aloud the verse they received from the Lord and commented on what it meant to them. No one asked me. I was not that important. But that night, my verse was etched into my soul, and I knew beyond any doubt that God had called me to "teach many to walk in righteousness," and one day, he would appoint me to that ministry.

It was still winter break when Nuți asked me to spend a week with her in the village of Dobra, where she had grown up. My parents consented, and I was excited to be in a home where everyone loved the Lord. We traveled by train, and Nuți's father came with us.

There were regions in Romania in which Protestantism penetrated deeper than in others. Dobra was such a village. It had a Baptist and a Pentecostal church, and many in that community were Repenters.

It was a white winter, and every day Nuți and I had a blast sledding down a steep hill and rolling about in the deep snow with some of the village kids. Nuți's aunt cooked for us while her father spent most of the day praying and reading the Bible. I had never seen anyone pray so much. Every time he left the house, he prayed at the door. Every time he arrived home, he stopped at the door and prayed again. Hours upon hours, he prayed, again and again. Before bed, Nuți and I usually read the Bible together and prayed, and after a few exchanges, we went to sleep.

---

1. Dan 12:3 NIV.

From Pain to Purpose

One night before I drifted off, I asked the Lord to speak to me through a dream if he had something he wanted to tell me. Around 4 a.m., I woke up suddenly with a strong feeling that I was supposed to intercede for someone. My father was the first person who came to mind. So, I prayed for his salvation until I drifted again to sleep.

In my dream that night, I was in a large, semi-lit room feeling down, as if no one cared about me. A girl from our church was also with me. Just then, there was a knock on the door. I recall feeling so insignificant that I was certain no one would be knocking for me. When my friend opened the door, I could see two men towering over her. They looked serious, and from their gestures, I could tell that they were in a rush and had no time to waste. To my surprise, they wanted to speak with me.

At the door, I stared at the two men, until one of them spoke, "We come on behalf of the Lord your God to bring you this." And with those words, he handed me a neatly folded scarf, smooth as the finest silk. It bore the color of the moonlit sky, with two large yellow stars in the top right-hand corner, surrounded by many smaller ones. I stared at the scarf in my hand and, as beautiful as it was, I couldn't help but wonder why God would send me a scarf, of all things. What did it mean, and what was I supposed to do with it?

I was about to ask the two men my questions, when suddenly, a thought, like a flash of lightning, rushed upon my mind, "This scarf is the verse from the book of Daniel: *'Those who are wise will shine like the brightness of the sky, and those who teach many to walk in righteousness like the stars forever and ever.'*"[2]

I looked at the two men, and they nodded their heads as if agreeing with my thoughts. No words were exchanged between us until the man who had spoken before spoke again.

"The Lord, your God, sent us to tell you that he heard your prayers, and you will be a missionary. Come and see."

A large screen appeared in front of me, and I saw myself on top of a dirt mound speaking to a group of people. For the next few

2. Dan 12:3 NIV.

The Call

moments, I tuned out everything around me and stared motionless at the image on the screen. Next to me, the two men looked as if they wanted to leave, when one of them turned and said:

"Oh, yes, the Lord your God also heard your prayer, and you will die for your faith. Come and see."

Immersed in my thoughts, I didn't even notice that the two men had disappeared. Then, in the blink of an eye, I was out of the vision and fully awake. The transition from sleep to consciousness was almost nonexistent as if the events had just happened in real life. I looked over to Nuți's bed and shouted, "Wake up! I had a dream! God told me that I would be a missionary!"

For the rest of the day, my body vibrated on and off until the evening. The next morning, we returned to the city—I with a twisted ankle and Nuți with a bruised back from a sledding accident, but our hearts were filled with the presence of God.

At this time, my father had found out that our church did not have an official license to gather as a congregation and met illegally at its present location. The government permitted only a limited number of Protestant churches to register so they could be easily monitored. All other churches were considered illegal. We were one of the largest underground churches in Romania.

On weekdays, many of us met in private homes for prayer, which was also against the law. So, my father threatened to close our church and send police officers to the houses to arrest us.

At this time, my sister became part of our youth group, and we prayed for her that she would soon show her commitment to Jesus publicly in baptism.

Within the harsh confines of communism, the decision to become a follower of Jesus was never undertaken as a private or halfway measure. The difference between those thoroughly committed to the faith and those who straddled the fence was that the committed ones were not afraid to profess Christ publicly in baptism and be persecuted.

From Pain to Purpose

At home, my father sensed that he was losing ground with my sister. He told her that she could go to church with me but that she could not be baptized. I don't think he believed that Dorina would listen to him because, one day, he pulled out the "big guns." He promised Dorina he would pay for her to have the biggest wedding with the most famous entertainers in the country if she was not baptized as a Repenter. My sister and I were both in the room when my father made Dorina the offer, and I knew he intended to hurt me simultaneously. My sister pretended not to hear him, and I couldn't have cared less.

Protestant churches in Romania held evangelistic services a couple of times a year, specifically for unbelievers. At those services, "the waters were stirred," and believers brought their unsaved friends and loved ones to church. The presence of the Lord was so weighty in those services, and the atmosphere was so prayer-filled, that nonbelievers didn't stand a chance. They wept out loud for their sins and made decisions for the Lord in hoards. I knew that an evangelistic service would soon take place at another Baptist church in our town, and I prayed that Dorina would go there with me.

When we arrived at the church, the courtyard was so crowded that she was swept away by a tidal wave of people rushing into the sanctuary. Throughout the entire service, I didn't know where she was. For two and a half hours, I prayed desperately that Dorina would hear the sermon and accept Christ as her Lord that night.

After the service, when I finally found her in the crowd, Dorina beamed with joy. She had raised her hand at the pastor's invitation and had given her life to the Lord. I was ecstatic. With two of us now in the home, I was sure that our family was on its way to being saved. My father saved? I was asking for a miracle indeed.

Soon after giving her life to the Lord, Dorina started to sew her baptism dress. It was a beautiful white satin with lace around the

The Call

neck and wrists, and I knew that she would look angelic in it. When she gave her testimony before the church, the head deacon asked me to stand next to my sister. After a long pause, trying to hold back his tears, he looked at me and said, "Your faithfulness... drew her in." The whole church wept with him.

Dorina's baptismal day arrived, and unlike me, she told my parents about it. My mother wanted to be there, and the three of us headed to church. The guest preacher that Sunday was none other than Pastor Petrică Dugulescu, the man whose sermon, two years earlier, led me to the Lord. He had moved permanently to our city to be the pastor of one of the registered Baptist churches, and since our little church didn't have a pastor, he occasionally preached at some of our services.

When the three of us left the house that morning, my father was quiet. He didn't lock the door behind us, nor did he answer when we said goodbye, and none of us could have imagined what was about to happen. Alone in the house, my father spent the entire morning sharpening the biggest slaughtering knife we owned, and for three hours, he planned how to plunge it into my sister's back when she came through the door, and then turn himself in.

When we entered the house, my father stood behind the door with his hand behind his back. But when he saw us and heard us laughing, he couldn't raise the knife. He ran into the kitchen and threw it into the sink, and then drank himself into a stupor.

Chapter 4

Faith in the Trenches

LIFE IN ROMANIA WAS deteriorating. Our country had become a prison for its people—a land of fears, poverty, and lies, where twenty-three million people had to either agree with the communist propaganda and blend in, or risk losing their remaining freedoms. Allegiance to anyone other than the dictator and the Communist Party was considered unpatriotic and had devastating consequences. Protestant Christians were brutalized, so the churches moved deeper underground.

One Sunday morning, when the service ended, I noticed several people whispering in the church courtyard. I caught up with my mentor to see if she knew what the secrecy was about. She had heard that an American evangelist named Billy Graham was coming to Romania. Our dictator wanted to dismiss the rumors that Protestants suffered under his regime, so he granted Billy Graham entrance into our "free" country under strict supervision.

Our youth group was frantic. We made plans to meet downtown to see the evangelist when he arrived in our city. Thousands of Christians and non-Christians gathered at the Orthodox Cathedral where Billy Graham was to speak. Due to the large crowds blocking the roads, all public transport in that direction had ceased.

Faith in the Trenches

After a long wait, a tall man emerged from a car and walked toward the cathedral, surrounded by several men in dark suits. He smiled, wanting to shake people's hands, but was shown brusquely to keep walking.

At that moment, Billy Graham did something every Romanian Protestant there understood, without a word being spoken. He raised his big Bible in the air and waved it over the crowd as if to say: "This book, which is now illegal in your country, will one day triumph over the lies that you are now forced to believe."

I tried to hold back my tears as I watched him disappear into the cathedral. Mr. Graham's interpreter was clearly an unbeliever who barely knew how to pronounce biblical names—an intentional attempt to weaken the evangelist's message. But outside the cathedral, no one left, even after the microphones were cut off. Protestants sang hymns while nonbelievers listened. Surrounding us from all directions, secret police officers in civilian clothing stood watch. The atmosphere felt heavy—perhaps a premonition of things to come.

Several of us from our youth group traveled to two other nearby cities where Mr. Graham spoke. His visit encouraged the persecuted churches of Romania. But most of all, it reminded us that our brothers and sisters in the free world had not forgotten about us.

Once a week, we continued to meet in our mentors' homes for prayer. With the doors locked and the windows covered, we spent hours in silent worship and intercession. Our prayers often resembled those of the believers in the book of Acts. We contended for boldness to bear witness at any cost and be ready to lay down our lives for our faith at any moment.

Week after week, we prayed the most outlandish prayers, asking God to open doors in Romania for the gospel to be preached in stadiums, city squares, on television, and on the radio. Every week we met under the cover of the night, held hands, sang, and prayed together.

From Pain to Purpose

But there was one prayer we never prayed in those house meetings. We never prayed for safety! For on the day we said yes to Christ, we also said yes to beatings, ridicule, imprisonment, and even death. To pray for safety would have been like saying: "Lord, I don't want to suffer for you." Safety and obedience to the Great Commission were not possible simultaneously, and we were well aware of that.

We also knew the words of Jesus that said: "Because of me, you will be brought before kings and governing authorities to serve as my witnesses." So, we prayed for strength and courage should that time come. But for me, that day came sooner than I thought.

I was sixteen years old, walking home from a youth gathering. A classmate from high school was with me. She was a troubled girl but with a soft heart. She often came to church with me and was on the verge of accepting the Lord.

About halfway home, a police officer stopped us and asked us to follow him to the station. I didn't realize when I left the church that I had forgotten to hide my Bible, and I carried it in my hand, in plain view. The communist regime had placed severe restrictions on printing and importing Bibles. And possessing or distributing any religious literature was considered a criminal offense.

The officer entered a block apartment that housed an undisclosed police station located on its bottom floor. We followed him inside. My friend whispered in my ear, begging me not to tell him that I was a Christian. But all I could think of at that moment was that this might be the only chance for this "governing authority" to hear the gospel. I had to say something.

The officer showed us into a back room, barely lit, with one chair facing a small desk. He sat down and asked me what I had in my hand. "So much for not telling him that I was a Christian!" I thought.

I handed him my Bible. He leafed through it and then asked matter-of-factly, "Who gave you this Bible?"

"I can't tell you, sir," I answered.

Faith in the Trenches

The officer looked up and asked the question again.

"Sir, I will answer truthfully any question that has to do with me, but I cannot tell you anything about anyone else," I said.

My friend clung to my arm, whimpering, and whispering in my ear not to make him mad. The officer left the room, and another officer walked in. He wasted no time reminding me that I risked never finishing high school and that he could send me to a correctional school for troubled teens if I did not cooperate.

Then, he calmly asked, "Who gave you this Bible?" He wanted names.

I looked at him and could almost hear my mentor's words: "Do not ever be a Judas. Do not ever betray your brothers in Christ, no matter the cost."

The officer waited for my answer while my friend kept elbowing me to give him the name so we could go home. I thought for a moment how deep into the woods and under pigpens, Christians hid hundreds of Bibles. Some of my friends risked their lives to transport those Bibles from the border. Would I become the weakest link in the chain and tell the officers what I knew? I couldn't do it.

The first officer came back into the room and tried to reason with me.

"Listen, you are a beautiful girl. Why are you wasting your time with religion? Only old, illiterate women believe in God anymore. If you really want to be religious, why don't you just go to the Orthodox cathedral? Why do you want to associate with an illegal sect?"

As he spoke, I saw my chance to share the gospel.

"I don't want to be religious, sir. What I have is not a religion but a relationship with God who wants a relationship with us."

I told the officers that God was good, and he loved them and gave his Son to die for their sins. As I spoke, they leafed through my Bible, pretending not to hear. They read out loud some of the prayers I had written on small pieces of paper and tucked between the pages. In one prayer, I had asked God to help me go to America to study the Bible at a Christian university.

From Pain to Purpose

America was considered the greatest enemy of communism and Romanians were forbidden to leave the country, especially to go to America. Armed forces and killer dogs heavily guarded our borders, and anyone who attempted to escape, if caught, was tortured, and sent to prison, without exception. My desire to go to America, written on that piece of paper, was enough evidence of intent to incriminate my entire family and me in a court of law. The officers read the prayer aloud and moved on as if they were entirely blind to its content.

Realizing that I would not cooperate, they told us to wait for them outside. They were coming to search our houses to look for more Christian materials. When my friend heard that, she began to sob uncontrollably.

I told the officers that my friend was not a Christian and had nothing to do with my Bible or the church. She was just visiting with me that evening. Protestant women in Romania were known for never wearing makeup or jewelry, so the big hoop earrings in my friend's ears and her heavy makeup were enough to convince them that I was telling the truth. They let my friend go and decided to search only my house. In communism, any law officer could enter anyone's house at any time and for any reason. No search warrant was required. It was almost midnight, and my parents didn't know where I was.

On our way to my house, I prayed desperately. I had so many books and copies of Christian books that people from church had given me. I knew I was going to be in trouble. But I didn't pray for myself. I was a minor, and in Romania, the parents of a minor were convicted or at least heavily fined whenever their child committed a crime. I didn't want my parents to be in trouble with the law for me. With every step, my prayers became more frantic. I needed God to intervene not tomorrow or later that day, but at that moment.

The officers walked slightly in front of me when suddenly one of them pointed at something on the sidewalk to our left. Beneath the dim streetlight, I could see the silhouette of a man walking beside his bicycle. One officer exclaimed, "He's carrying an ax!"

Faith in the Trenches

We lived in a large university city. People didn't usually carry pickaxes with them on the street. This took precedence over my house search, and the officers decided to follow the man instead. I was suddenly left alone in the middle of the street and didn't know if I should wait for them to return, or I should leave. Just then, one of the officers turned and said hurriedly, "Go home!" As I walked away, I realized that not at any point had I given them my address or my full name.

When I rang the bell, my mother opened the door. She looked furious and was worried about me. But she became even more furious when I told her that the police had interrogated me for the last two hours for carrying a Bible. She slapped me across the face and shouted, "Why can't you just be normal like other Christians who don't talk about Jesus all the time and get themselves into trouble with the police?"

Then, she rushed into my bedroom and threw on the floor every Christian book and piece of paper that could be incriminating in a court of law. She bagged everything, and early the following morning, took the bag to a friend of hers who lived nearby. Weeks and months had passed. Our house was never searched.

But my mother was right. I was not "normal" like other Christians. I don't know why, but I couldn't keep my mouth shut, even if I had to take a beating for it occasionally. I didn't deliberately try to get myself into trouble, but I couldn't be silent when I felt I needed to speak. There was so much pain around me. People needed hope that was found only in Jesus. Someone had to tell them the good news. If not I, then who?

Although street evangelism and proselytizing were illegal in Romania, I looked every day for people whom God might want to touch through me on the street. I had an unquenchable desire to witness, and the opportunities multiplied.

Sometimes, I would offer to help older people with their baggage, and I would tell them about the Lord on the way to their house. I was also in the habit of buying extra bus or tram tickets.

From Pain to Purpose

If the conductor came and someone had forgotten theirs, I would quickly slip it to them, and when they thanked me, I would tell them about Jesus who paid the price for them. Still others on the street, I approached directly and invited them to church. I was young and nonthreatening. People were invariably curious to hear what I had to say.

My witness especially moved the older women. It was unusual in Romania for a young city girl to start a conversation about God. Some even came to church with me. Only in eternity would I know the rest. The important thing was that the seed was planted. It was up to God to take it from there and make it grow. Yet, there was one incident that taught me a lesson I would not soon forget.

I was walking home one afternoon when an older lady on the sidewalk in front of me struggled to carry her bags. I felt the presence of the Lord come upon me, urging me to help her and tell her that he loved her.

Usually, when the Lord sent me on one of those witnessing assignments, I could feel his presence rising inside of me as a gentle tingling that filled me with joy and boldness, showing me exactly what to do. I loved street evangelism, and God gave me a particular grace and zeal for it at that time. I hurried to catch up with the lady in front of me, eager to help her and tell her that God loved her. But when I caught a glimpse of her face, I stopped in my tracks.

"But Father, she's a Gypsy!" I blurted to God and myself all at once.

No sooner had those words formed into my mind when instantly I felt the presence of God depart from me, leaving me with a hollow feeling inside. There was no rebuke, just a sudden and brutal removal of God's presence.

As a child, I feared the Gypsies. They walked the streets in dirty clothes, selling pots and pans and wooden spoons they had often stolen. My mother sometimes threatened to give me to the Gypsies when I was not a good girl. So, I would run inside and hide whenever I saw their caravans coming down the street. As I grew older, I avoided Gypsies altogether. The shock that God

Faith in the Trenches

would have me speak to a Gypsy was so great that I could not filter my emotions, not even before God.

When the palpable presence of God left me, I thought that my hesitation to obey right away had displeased him. I tried to recover by quickly starting a conversation with the woman. But my initial excitement to witness turned into drudgery. I carried the woman's bags to the upper floor of a nearby building where she lived. When we arrived at her door, she thanked me, and I delivered my usual message, saying, "Jesus loves you so much. Do you know who he is?" Appearing eager to go inside, and probably having detected my lack of enthusiasm, she said politely, "Yes, I know." I turned around, feeling like a massive failure. I didn't want politeness. I wanted "fruit that remained!"

As I pondered the incident over the years, it finally hit me that not all was lost that day. For all I knew, the woman may have already been a Christian and simply needed to hear that the Lord loved her and then go on about her day. After all, that was the only message the Lord wanted me to give her. But whether or not she was a believer, that encounter taught me two valuable lessons. First, that God had zero tolerance for prejudice and has no problem withdrawing his presence from anyone who harbors such tendency; and second, that any ministry devoid of God's presence was rarely fruitful and never joyful. God had exposed an ugly sin in my life that day, but it took years before I fully understood it and repented of it.

Over the following months, I continued to witness at home, at school, and on the streets, and in my quiet time, the Lord continued to solidify my call to ministry.

Cristian, the young man who entered my life, also had a radical conversion, including receiving the mantle of intercession and the call to pastoral ministry. There was rarely a day that he and I did not meet to intercede for some purpose or person. We often fasted together, especially for each other's unbelieving parents.

From Pain to Purpose

Sometimes, on Sundays, we took the train to different village churches that had no pastors. There, Cristian preached, and I sang and played my guitar. We were ecstatic when the first person gave his life to the Lord at Cristian's sermon, and we dreamed of continuing this mission together for the rest of our lives.

Cristian was two years older than me, and after graduating from high school, he reported for his mandatory year-and-a-half military service. The fact that he was a Christian meant that he would probably spend most of that time in a labor camp where prisoners, political dissidents, and Repenters worked to dig a canal that connected the Danube River to the Black Sea.

During this period, when Cristian was away, I sensed the Lord inviting me into a deeper life of prayer and intercession. At school, I often sat alone during recess and prayed for all my classmates by name. During my one-hour walk home, I prayed along the way, and then again later in my room I prayed for several more hours before bed. As I look back, I yearn for that gift of prayer again. But my favorite thing was when my whole family left the house, and I could pray out loud in different rooms, uninterrupted.

One day, when everyone was away, I knelt by a chair in the living room. I liked that I didn't have to whisper my prayers, so I began to intercede with loud cries. I prayed for my family and contended before the Lord for my classmates, teachers, and our country. My prayer became so intense and warfare-like that suddenly, in the middle of a sentence, I uttered words I didn't understand, and when I did, something like an electrical current went through my body.

I had a general knowledge about spiritual gifts from Scripture, but no one in my Baptist church had ever explained how they might manifest in real life. I didn't know if the gift of tongues was still operative today and, if so, then for what purpose. I had no framework for understanding.

When the strange words bolted from my mouth, I stopped praying and said out loud, "Lord, what was *that*?" I thought that my agonizing prayer somehow caused my words to slip into nonsense and that I needed to dial it down. So, I dismissed the experience as something weird and decided not to mention it to a living soul.

Soon after that incident, our youth leader married a young woman from a Pentecostal church in town. As a result, our youth groups became friends, and we often met for prayer, exchanged songs, and went together on retreats into the mountains. The more time I spent with those Pentecostal teens, the more I wanted what they had. I couldn't put my finger on exactly what that was, but they seemed so much more on fire for the Lord than we Baptists were, and I envied them for that.

On one occasion, one of their leaders explained to me that their passion for the Lord came from their relationship with the Holy Spirit, who gives gifts to empower us in our weaknesses and build up the church. I never heard anyone speak about having a relationship with the Holy Spirit, but it struck me as important enough that I, too, desired it with my whole heart.

One Sunday, after the morning service, a few of us went to the hospital to visit the sick and then gathered in a park to pray until the evening service. On the bench, I asked one of the Pentecostal young men to pray for me to be filled with the Holy Spirit and receive the gift of tongues. He prayed for several minutes, but nothing happened, and I was unsure what to think about that.

A few months later, in the middle of something mundane, I was suddenly struck by a thought that connected what had happened to me in the living room when I prayed and the gift of tongues. "What if the two events were ostensibly one and the same thing?" I wondered. It didn't take long before the Lord confirmed in my heart that I already had the gift, and I should begin using it in prayer.

My passion for the Lord continued to deepen, and I became even bolder in my witness. Through his Word and dreams, God reconfirmed my calling to preach the gospel, and I continued to pray that one day he would send me to America to study the Bible at a Christian university. I heard my mentors pray so often for impossible things for our country, so why not pray for what seemed impossible for my own life?

From Pain to Purpose

I was so excited about my calling to ministry that I shared it with just about everyone I knew. Unfortunately, not all shared in my excitement. My parents were concerned that the wrong people would hear me talking about wanting to go to America and arrest all of us. But to my surprise, I encountered the harshest opposition to my calling from within the church.

I had confided in a girl from our youth group that I believed I would someday go to America to study the Bible at a Christian school. She scoffed and reminded me of the well-known Romanian proverb: "pasărea mălai visează," which means "every bird dreams of seeds." The implication was that dreaming about something doesn't mean it will happen. Sadly, the women of the church showed the strongest disapproval of my enthusiasm to preach the gospel.

One day I visited our children's minister to talk with her about this. I wanted to speak with her specifically because she seemed more open-minded. Whenever English-speaking preachers came to our church, she was their interpreter. She appeared confident speaking in front of people, and I admired her behind the pulpit.

I spent almost two hours sharing my joy about my calling with her, as I came to understand it. She listened quietly, and I couldn't wait to hear her thoughts. Then, the levy broke. She started by firing rebukes at me for wanting to rise above men's authority in the church. She called my desire to preach not only prideful and unbiblical but potentially demonic. For, just as Satan sought to rise above God's authority, so was I, she said, seeking to rise above men's established authority. She insinuated that my very salvation could not be genuine if I believed that God would go against his own Word to call a woman to preach the gospel. Her last words to me were a grave admonition:

"Go home and repent, and maybe God will forgive you of your pride."

All the way home, I tried to keep from crying. I was devastated. I didn't want to usurp any man's authority. All women in Romania, Christian and non-Christian, knew their roles in society quite well, and none ever challenged those roles, especially in the church. Besides, I had never so much as seen a woman pastor in my life. I didn't even know that they existed. All I felt was a call to share the gospel, and what I needed from her was a word of encouragement. Instead, I left her house questioning my very salvation.

Back in my room, I tried to process what had happened. Everything God promised me in the last four years was slowly crumbling under the weight of that woman's words. I closed my eyes and tried to imagine myself doing something else with my life, maybe getting married and having a little "girly" job. The very thought of it made me furious, and I began to cry.

Why wasn't I "normal" like the other girls in my church? Why did I feel this way? Why was the Word of God burning in my bones and I had to preach or die? Was it not the Lord who had led me to believe that he wanted me to "teach many to walk in righteousness"? Or did Satan surreptitiously put that idea inside my head? Did my flesh desire it out of some rebelliousness against God? Do unsaved women dream about preaching Jesus? Is that even possible?

For the first time, I was confused about God's plan for my life. I was seventeen years old, and when I thought about my future, I saw nothing, like staring at a blank wall. I felt disoriented and hopeless and began to mourn the loss of a future I never had, except in my dreams. If this woman was right, how could I have been so deceived?

Chapter 5

Dress Rehearsal

THE SUMMER OF 1988 brought on a whirlwind. I graduated from high school, and Cristian, my boyfriend of four years, asked me to marry him. His parents had given their consent, and Cristian's father had procured a set of jeweler's bands for me to try on for size for my custom-made wedding ring.

Culturally, Romanian Christians didn't "date around." When a couple dated, it was commonplace to talk about their marriage and plan their forthcoming wedding. Since dating almost always guaranteed marriage, engagements were significant family events and never surprises or private affairs. Cristian's marriage proposal simply meant that his family could proceed to order the rings, and both families could meet and set a date for the engagement and wedding days.

Cristian's eyes beamed with expectation when we talked about our marriage, and in my heart, I was as excited as he was. I remembered the day we walked along the Bega River, before Cristian went into the national service, when he asked me to promise that I would wait for him, and we would marry as soon as he returned. We held hands under a honeysuckle tree, and I promised him that I would.

Dress Rehearsal

He was the first man I ever loved, and I wanted to spend the rest of my life with him. Everything seemed perfect for us to take that step, including the fact that Cristian felt called to be a pastor, and I wanted more than anything in the world to marry a pastor.

Yet, the thought of marriage also caused me intense apprehension. I had my own call to ministry, and I feared that marrying so young would hinder me from fulfilling that calling. Cristian had always encouraged me to believe in my gifting, but, as a married couple, it went without saying that my calling would be secondary to his calling, and my ministry dependent upon his, because I was a woman. I yearned for so much more out of life than simply being married.

But there was something else that gave me serious pause about marrying Cristian. He was irrationally jealous. We couldn't walk anywhere without his questioning me as to which way my eyes turned. He often accused me of returning the affection of a guy in our youth group behind his back. That person was his best friend, Ştefan. Even telling God in prayer that I loved him sent Cristian into a fit of jealousy.

Many a time he sent me back into the house to change what I was wearing if he thought my clothes could attract the attention of another man. During the day, he phoned excessively to check where I was and wanted us to be together every waking hour.

One autumn day, Cristian took the scarf I wore around my neck and wrapped it around my head and face like a burka, leaving only my eyes showing. "I wish you wore it like this every time you went outside, so no man looked at you," he said. Then, teary-eyed, he grasped me by the shoulders and added, "I love you so much. You are mine. Do you understand? I wish I could keep you in a cage, so I'm the only man who looks at you. You belong to me and no one else."

He made that statement quite often, and I resented it. It frightened me. It sounded possessive and made me feel like property. I was afraid that his jealousy might drive him to violence someday if I were to marry him. His constant suspicions caused us to argue all the time, and everyone in our youth group grew tired of it, including me. But Cristian insisted that his jealousy would subside, and we would not argue like this once we got married. So, despite the tension, quarreling, and uncertainty that defined our relationship, Cristian's family proceeded to order the wedding bands.

My nagging doubts about our future marriage mounted, even though we continued to minister together in the villages. But it wasn't long before Cristian felt drawn to the youth ministry of a larger church in town and sought to convince me to join him there. I loved our little church and had no desire to leave it. It was my home.

By the time winter came, our relationship had crumbled. I needed a break to think more clearly about how my call to ministry and our marriage could work together. Unfortunately, I didn't know how to articulate those feelings to Cristian or anyone else. When he refused to grant me space to think, I broke up with him, and that day a part of me shattered into a thousand pieces.

Cristian continued to call me, asking that we start over. But I wasn't ready. When he insisted, I invented a story that I was in love with his best friend, Ștefan, the guy he suspected me of liking.

I was not attracted to Ștefan, but I knew that he liked me, which made it easy for us to begin dating. I hoped that Cristian's seeing me with Ștefan would keep him at a distance and give me enough time to sort out my thoughts. Every bit of my plan was illogical, immature, and culturally taboo, but I didn't know what else to do. I didn't expect my relationship with Ștefan to last. At best, I expected it to move slowly, but to my dread, Ștefan was falling in love with me, and I didn't know how to stop it. Even my parents, who never interfered in those matters, expressed their shock and disapproval at the way I was using Ștefan and at my deplorable love triangulation.

Every day, Cristian would follow me from the distance to and from work. Then one day, he shouted from the top of his lungs in the middle of the street: "I love a girl, but she doesn't love me!" Far

Dress Rehearsal

down the boulevard, everyone could hear him. I pretended not to know him.

On the rare occasions that we did talk, Cristian would always say, "If you want it, God still does," meaning our relationship. But this failed to help his cause. It made me feel like I was the rebellious one, while he was clearly on God's side.

I felt confused and lonely throughout it all, with no one to help me sort out my feelings. Even our mutual mentor and close friends spoke to me on Cristian's behalf, hoping I'd change my mind. Yet, no one asked how I felt about it. So, the more they pushed, the more I stubbornly backed away.

A few months later, after several failed attempts to reconcile, Cristian got engaged to a girl from another church, and Ștefan and I received an invitation to their wedding. I was both relieved and wrecked beyond words.

After graduating from high school, I worked as a secretary for my father's brother—the staunch atheist. He held a top CEO position at a renowned heavy-machinery industry in our city. He took a chance on hiring me even though I was a Christian, hoping that the corporate world would lure me away from my faith, as he later admitted.

I worked in an office full of lawyers, engineers, and economists. And, since my uncle and I had the same last name, the company lavished me with undue attention, including large bonuses throughout the year.

I loved working there, but in my heart, I yearned for so much more. I dreamed of studying the Bible in America, and when I closed my eyes at night, I could see myself preaching to the masses in stadiums. Then, I'd pray, "Lord, how will this ever come to pass?" And the Lord would gently remind me about the doors that he opens that no one can shut.

From Pain to Purpose

The Romanian economy was at a breaking point. People and animals were starving, and every gesture of free expression was subject to extermination. Misery was at every turn, despite the government's propaganda that we lived in a "golden era" and that we had never lived better. For those who dared to disagree, their fate fell squarely upon their heads. So, Christians everywhere fasted and prayed for God to deliver us from evil.

In January 1989, several of us from our youth group formed a prayer chain. We each chose a day of the week to fast and pray on that day for a year for our country. I didn't mind that my day for fasting fell on a Sunday, but my parents were furious. Not eating the Sunday meal for an entire year was preposterous to them. But for my father, what was even more preposterous was that anyone would believe that a solid communist government like ours would "magically" disappear just because a handful of kids refused to eat and went on "talking to themselves," which was my father's definition of prayer. My sister also fasted with us. We were both strong believers, but somehow, my father seemed angry only with me, and his anger came in waves.

One evening after dinner, my sister was sitting next to me at the table. For some reason, my father decided that day to tell me exactly how he felt about me.

"I am so ashamed of what you had become that I never talk about you with any of my friends or coworkers. To me, you don't even exist. You are dead!" he said, emphasizing every word.

He could have said the same thing about my sister, but he didn't. For to him, I was the ringleader, the one who had brought this Christian plague upon our house. In his mind, my sister was simply too weak to resist. So, it was I who usually took the brunt of his fury. But on that day, his words cut like a knife, and I burst into tears right in front of him. I didn't understand why he was so ashamed of me. I wasn't perfect, but I was polite and helped around the house. I didn't smoke or drink or curse or lie. I was a virgin, and I was beautiful. With virtues that would make most fathers proud of their daughters, it was painful to hear those words come from my father's mouth.

Dress Rehearsal

The seven of us who committed to fasting for a year met weekly in our mentor's apartment for prayer and intercession. A mix of Baptists and Pentecostals, mostly teenagers, we came together to plead before the Lord for our country.

Each time we met, we prayed for several hours until one day, the presence of God came powerfully among us in the middle of our intercession. Suddenly, a Baptist girl began to prophesy. She had never done so before. Within her spirit, she saw the map of Romania unfolding before her eyes, and from our city of Timișoara, blood gushed as from an open wound, spreading in different directions across the country. One after another, cities became open wounds until blood covered the whole map.

When the vision ended, we fell on our faces on the floor before God. We believed he had shown us the future to prepare us for a coming bloodbath for Christians in Romania, starting in our city. We prayed until late in the evening, and when we left the gathering, we had made up our minds that, whatever might happen, we would endure to the end.

That summer, I heard through a secret source that a group of pastors had formed an underground seminary in our city. Interested students could interview on a particular day at an obscure location. I knew the place, and wild horses would not have stopped me from showing up that day. A seminary was universally understood to be a school that trained male students for pastoral ministry, although there was no explicit mention of it in this instance.

Several women accompanied their husbands or boyfriends to that location that day, but I was there to interview, and I was not about to be deterred. I wanted to study the Bible so badly that I was determined to do just about anything short of disguising myself as a man to be accepted.

After a long wait, at last, they called my name. I entered a room in which two Baptist pastors sat at a table facing the door.

From Pain to Purpose

One was Pastor Petrică Dugulescu. The other was also a pastor in town who knew me from ministering with Cristian in the same village where he also ministered.

As I stood across the table from them, one of the pastors asked, "Lumi, what do you believe about speaking in tongues?"

My heart dropped. These were Baptist pastors. If they didn't deny my admission because I was a woman, I felt certain they would reject me if I told them that I spoke in tongues. I hesitated for a moment and then said:

"I believe the gift of tongues is real. I believe that the Holy Spirit gives us that gift. When I received it, I was so happy that you could have given me the most expensive car in exchange for that joy, and I would not have given it up."

They thanked me and asked me to wait in the hallway until they announced those admitted. The entire interview lasted less than two minutes. "Was that all there was to be of my entrance exam?" I wondered. If so, I couldn't believe that I had blown my only chance to become a seminary student. If they had asked me anything else related to the Bible, I surely would have passed.

Someone interviewed before me was asked to summarize the seventeenth chapter of the Gospel of Mark. When he responded by saying that Mark had only sixteen chapters, they all laughed, which ostensibly meant that he had passed. I knew my Bible. If they had asked me that same question, I would have given the same answer. But, alas, I consoled myself for being truthful about speaking in tongues.

When the first round of interviews concluded, the pastors came into the hallway to announce the acceptances. When I heard my name, I could barely hold back a scream. Other women, having seen that I was admitted, asked for an interview in the second round. I was glad to see that they, too, had passed. I would not be the sole female student at the new seminary.

We learned when classes were to begin, and I thought that I had died and gone to heaven. I didn't care if I studied the Bible in a Romanian seminary or an American one. I was happy wherever

Dress Rehearsal

I was afforded the opportunity, and now it was in my own city of Timișoara.

Every week we attended lectures in the New and Old Testaments, in homiletics, church history, and English—until one day we arrived at the seminary only to find the doors locked, with no explanation. Someone among us must have been an informant, because the secret police had found us.

The Baptist pastors had been interrogated and asked to turn in a list with the names of all the students enrolled in the seminary. When they refused, the officials ordered that the seminary be closed. In time, they would have closed us anyway.

Communist Romania had only one television station. All media was controlled and censored by the government. But very late at night, one could faintly hear radio broadcasts from West Germany in the Romanian language. Listening to those stations was illegal and the penalty for doing so was a lengthy prison sentence. Yet many took that chance because true news under the communist regime was in short supply.

It was by those broadcasts that we heard of the fall of communism in Czechoslovakia and Poland earlier that year. Then in October, communism collapsed in Hungary, and in November, the wall came down in East Germany. By early December, an uneasy air could be felt hovering over Romania. Something was brewing under the surface and was about to erupt. Romanians could no longer hide the feeling of having had enough.

Chapter 6

Truth Sends to Prison

THE LONG COMMUTE FROM work made the afternoon seem to drag on forever. I stared mindlessly out of the dirty window of the tram, trying to ignore the screech of the metal wheels grinding against the tracks. Station after station, everything looked the same: the same grey buildings, the same dusty streets, and the same hopeless look on everyone's face.

Christmas was almost a week away, and the city swarmed with people hunting for a few morsels of food for the holidays. As hard as communism had tried to erase God from the soul of our nation, it was futile. Faith was etched within us for two millennia. So, year after year, all Romanians, Christians and atheists alike, secretly observed Christmas.

The tram pulled into Maria Station, and something outside the window caught my eye. A group of people stood in front of the Hungarian Reformed church next to the station. Large street gatherings were forbidden in communism unless organized and monitored closely by the Communist Party. From inside the tram, everyone stared out the window, but no one said a word.

Truth Sends to Prison

When I arrived home, I ran into the kitchen where my father was eating. If anyone knew anything about an illegal gathering, it would be my father.

"Tati, I saw people gathered in front of the Reformed Church at Maria Station. Do you know anything about it?" I asked in one breath.

It was a warm December day, and the kitchen window was open. My father walked over to close it. It was his signal that what he was about to tell me was for my ears only.

"The pastor of that Reformed church is a troublemaker," my father said. "He has had problems repeatedly with the secret police for speaking out against communism. Instead of sticking to the Bible, he preached about human rights abuses in Romania—things that were none of his business to talk about. They warned him several times to stop his capitalist agenda, but he refused. Now, he deserves what's coming to him."

"He deserves what's coming to him? What will they do to him?" I asked.

"Well, he is a Hungarian. They probably won't do too much to him publicly. But they cut off his lights and boarded his windows when he refused to leave the parsonage. I heard that they beat him and pushed around his child and pregnant wife. He has no way of getting food or water. Eventually, he will have to come out. He should have kept his mouth shut!"

I felt sick to my stomach. I couldn't believe how callously my father saw the situation. With every word that he uttered fury rose inside me. I put my coat back on and headed toward the front door, screaming:

"How long will they treat us like animals? How long will they do to us whatever they want?"

I didn't care if anyone heard me in the next building or down the avenue. My father just stared at me. I slammed the door and struck out for the church. For the first time, it hit me squarely between the eyes that my father's loyalty would never rest with anyone else but the Communist Party.

From Pain to Purpose

I met Ștefan at church, and when the service ended, I told him that I didn't want to go home. I wanted to see what was going on at the Reformed pastor's house. We arrived at Maria Station and walked toward the church. There, the crowd had grown, and the people seemed restless. We stood with them for a long time in silent solidarity until, suddenly, some men began to shout, "Freedom! Down with communism!"

I froze. "We are dead!" I thought to myself. "No one will leave this place alive. Those words alone are enough to put all of us in front of a firing squad."

I looked at Ștefan, and I was in even greater shock. His fist was up in the air, and he was chanting with the crowd the pastor's name: "Laslo Tokes! Laslo Tokes! Down with communism! Down with Ceaușescu!"

Ștefan must have seen the terrified look in my eyes because he stopped and whispered in my ear, "This is getting dangerous. We should go home."

I looked at him and I knew what he intended to do. He would take me home and then come back alone. I was scared to be there, but I didn't want to go home. "If we are writing history right now, I'm going to be part of it!" I said to myself.

For the next few minutes, the crowd grew louder and more restless. I knew that this was bigger than I was, bigger than all of us, and more dangerous than anything anybody had ever attempted, but I couldn't go home. My heart was with the people. Their cry was my cry. Their pain was my own.

Ștefan knew better than to insist on taking me home. So, he suggested that we go to his buddy's house nearby and leave our Bibles and my handbag there.

"If we need to run, our hands will be free," Ștefan said.

I left my purse at his friend's house, but I couldn't part with my little Bible. I slipped it unnoticed into my coat pocket, and we went back to join the crowd. At the Reformed church, the protest was in full swing. People were shouting unrestrained anti-communist

Truth Sends to Prison

slogans, shaking their fists in the air. We did the same. There was no turning back. We were finally saying out loud what we had been forbidden to think of, for decades.

Around midnight, fire trucks came against us, spraying us, trying to disperse us. We scattered behind buildings, only to return to the pastor's house an even larger crowd. A man called out to us to stay united and not give up, declaring that the victory was ours. He motioned to follow him downtown, which was a short walk over the Bega River. We marched peacefully across the bridge when, suddenly, screams burst forth from the front of the line. People turned and ran in every direction. Ştefan grabbed my hand, and we hid in the bushes behind a nearby building.

A specialized unit of antiriot police in white uniforms and large body shields invaded the crowd, beating people with thick rubber sticks. For a moment, it looked as if we were on a movie set where the script had gone horribly wrong. People ran chaotically from the police, and some were being beaten in front of us.

Despite the unit's intimidating appearance, the crowd resisted and soon overtook the troops. A few strong men lifted the police vehicle and pushed it over the bridge and into the river. Someone shattered a nearby bookstore window, and within minutes, all the dictator's books were being tossed into a fire. Downtown, we stood on the steps of the beautiful Moldavian Gothic-style cathedral, holding hands, and singing old patriotic songs, some of which had been forbidden in the "golden era."

Around two o'clock in the morning, we headed toward the student dormitories. As we marched and chanted, apartment lights came on, one after another. People in pajamas appeared at their windows, smiling, and waving jubilantly at the crowd. We motioned them to join us. Many came running as if they had been waiting a lifetime for this moment. On our way to the student dorms, we nearly doubled our numbers, and our voices became a thundering force.

Then, tragedy struck. From my left, an unmarked car drove at full speed, headlong into the throng of marchers. One person was severely hurt. But nothing stopped the crowd. We crossed the entire city, protesting, and by four o'clock that morning, we were a force to be reckoned with.

My feet started to hurt in the high-heeled boots I had worn for church, and I was exhausted. Over the long hours of running and protesting, fear had accumulated inside me and turned into a full-blown panic attack I had never experienced before. I could barely breathe. So, Ștefan and I turned from the crowd and sat on a bench in a park to rest.

I had just caught my breath when, in the distance, we spotted a detachment of soldiers heading in our direction. Ștefan and I looked at each other but were too tired to even try to run. I closed my eyes and, for a moment, pretended that it was all a bad dream.

The platoon stopped in front of us. The commander took off his machine gun, resting it on his boot. We watched him motionless. These soldiers were young, just like us, some barely out of high school. Will they pull the trigger? That night, anything could happen.

The officer asked for our IDs. He wanted to know what we were doing in the park at that hour of the night. Ștefan explained that I was sick and couldn't breathe. The commander ordered us to leave immediately. I felt panic coming back, and I gasped for air. Ștefan was concerned that I couldn't walk, so, we hesitated to leave. The officer then raised his weapon and struck Ștefan across the shoulder with the butt of his gun. "I told you to scat. Didn't you hear me?"

I reached for Ștefan's hand, and we left trying to decide whether we should go home or straight to church for the Christmas rehearsals that were to start at eight o'clock that morning. If we walked to church we could arrive on time. But what will I tell my parents? They must be sick with worry by now. I had never been out all night without letting them know where I was.

I decided I would deal with that later, so we started our long trek to church. Public transport was not yet running, and whenever we heard a car approaching, we hid inside a block apartment until it passed.

Truth Sends to Prison

We made our way behind the Bega store when suddenly a van turned the corner sharply and sped toward us. We pressed our backs against a building, hoping not to be seen. But they had already seen us. There was nowhere to go, nowhere to hide. The van stopped. A man jumped out, grabbed Ştefan by the arm, and dragged him into the car.

From inside the van, another man shouted, "Take the girl too!"

I walked to the car, and the man pushed me in next to Ştefan. Inside the van, the back seats faced each other, and in front of us sat three officers in civilian clothing. I leaned closer to Ştefan and whispered in his ear, "We tell them the truth. Yes?" Ştefan nodded.

One of the officers looked intently at me. "So, what were you doing out this early in the morning?" he asked.

"We were at the protest," I answered.

The officers looked at each other, trying not to laugh. Even they thought it was stupid to admit to such a crime.

"You mean, you were not at a party like all the others we've picked up all night?"

"No! We protested all night," I replied.

As Christians, we couldn't lie, even if lying would have given us back our freedom. We were at the protest, and we told them so. The officers seemed to wonder if we were plain dumb or just pretended to be dumb for some reason.

No one spoke until the driver asked in a loud voice, "Where to, Comrades?"

"Popa Şapcă," the officer who sat staring at me answered.

"No! This can't be true. I am tired, and I'm hallucinating," I thought.

Popa Şapcă was the nickname of the largest maximum-security prison in western Romania. "Please, Lord, don't let this be true," I prayed. "No one in my family had ever been to 'pârnaie.' What had I done?"

Romanian dissidents ordinarily were tried and convicted as criminals in military courts. But in exceptional circumstances such as participating in a popular uprising or instigating an anti-communist protest, prisoners could be executed immediately for high treason, without even a right to trial.

Frozen in my seat, I stared outside the window. When the van stopped, the massive prison gates opened before us. One of the officers said to the guard at the gate, "These two confessed. Put them with the *special* crowd."

"If they confessed once, they would confess again. They'll go with the others," the prison guard replied sharply.

Outside the van, Ștefan held me in a protective grip, softly kissing my hair. A guard rushed over and pulled us apart. He took Ștefan to the men's side of the prison. Another guard led me to the women's side.

As I walked away, guarded, I heard someone shout my name, "Lumi! I love you!"

I turned and saw the guard shoving Ștefan forward toward a barrack. I couldn't bear to watch. I took a few steps and again heard my name. "Lumi! I'm praying for you!"

I forced myself not to look back. Ștefan's voice pierced the night.

The guard escorted me to a tiny building and told me to wait in line outside to be searched. I leaned closer, hoping to hear what they asked the women in front of me, but I was too far back. The line moved slowly, and my feet felt numb in my high heels.

As I waited, I peered around the courtyard with unnatural curiosity. Massive stone walls hovered over the grey buildings, and the sparse flickering lights made me feel as if I was trapped inside a medieval fortress. Prison guards, like dark shadows, rushed around the courtyard, and I could hear shouts echoing from the surrounding buildings.

My teeth chattered, so I buried my face in my coat collar. Then, for the first time that night, I slipped my hands into my pockets. Suddenly, I realized that I had my Bible with me. I had forgotten about it, and I knew that they would find it. In communism, the Bible was a Christian's most prized possession, and I

Truth Sends to Prison

feared they would make it a point to destroy it right in front of me. I couldn't let that happen.

The line started to move faster, and it was almost my turn to be searched. I gripped the Bible in my pocket, praying for a miracle but preparing for the worst. Suddenly, inside the pocket, I felt a small hole. Trying not to be noticed, I started to rip the stitches with my fingers and knuckles, making the hole big enough to slip my Bible through it. As I stepped forward, the Bible fell through the hole, inside the lining of my long coat. When I arrived at the officer's desk, I had to hand over all possessions I had with me. My pockets were empty, and my hands were free. So far as they could tell, I had nothing on me.

A male guard escorted two other women and me to a building across the courtyard. Inside, we walked a long corridor and stopped in front of cell number thirteen. A woman guard met us there and opened the three massive doors of the cell. First a wooden door, then a foot-thick metal one, and lastly, a door made entirely of iron bars. The three doors shut loudly behind us.

Inside the cell, to my left and right, were two bunk beds completely bare. In the back of the cell were a wooden bench, a sink, and a toilet behind a busted door. On the wall to my right, a wooden plank served as a shelf holding a few well-worn books.

The two women and I looked at each other stunned. They were both in their early twenties, and I was nineteen. We introduced ourselves, when one of them, a Hungarian, began to cry. In broken Romanian, she tried to tell us that she and her boyfriend had been kissing outside the student dormitory when a police car stopped and seized them. Frightened, she could barely find her words. The other girl was named Sorina, and she also began to cry.

I stared at the floor, processing as best as I could the events of the past twelve hours and how quickly they had escalated. But now, inside that prison cell, there was only one thing I could do. I asked my prison mates if they wanted to pray with me. Sorina said that she had never prayed in her life and didn't know how.

From Pain to Purpose

The Hungarian girl was so distraught that she didn't understand a word I said.

I can't remember what I prayed, but when I opened my eyes both women were sobbing. I looked at their tear-soaked faces and said to them: "The greatest cry of your hearts, God will count it as prayer." With that, silence fell upon the room.

Through a small, barred window, high up near the ceiling, I could see that it was now daylight. Outside the door, there was a commotion, and a few minutes later, the guards pushed two other young women into our cell.

More women were thrown in over the next few hours, with large bruises on their backs and faces. By evening, nineteen of us were packed into the likes of a closet. We had had no food or water the entire day. The only things allowed from the outside were cigarettes, and soon, dizzying clouds of nicotine filled the small cell, making it barely possible to see each other for the smoke.

An officer stopped briefly in front of our cell to check roll. When he heard my last name, he asked, "Are you, by any chance, related to the CEO of the heavy-machinery factory?"

"Yes, he is my uncle. I'm also his secretary," I said.

"Well, I guess Uncle will have to go without his little coffee now," the officer said sarcastically before slamming the door.

Around nine o'clock that evening, the two outer doors of the cell opened. At the base of the barred door left closed, almost unnoticeable, was an opening through which they passed the prisoners' food. One by one, the hungry women grabbed their plates and began eating some mushy boiled cabbage that smelled as bad as it looked. I watched with disgust the scene unfolding before me.

I was not a criminal, to be kept behind iron bars. Nor was I a dangerous animal to be shoveled mush through a feeding hole. I was a young woman who asked for the basic things of life: food, heat, and the freedom to speak and believe as I desired. Was that too much to ask of a civilized society?

Truth Sends to Prison

I took the plate handed to me through the hole and found a place on the floor to sit. Then, I lowered my head to pray, and when I opened my eyes, I let out a scream. Hundreds of maggots crawled out of my plate and onto my hand.

"Stop eating! There are maggots in the food!" I shouted.

Some women felt instantly nauseous. Others shrieked and began hitting the door with their fists and feet. I was afraid that sending back the food would be taken as a hunger strike, putting us in even graver trouble. So, I suggested that we toss the food in the sink and the toilet. We watched, until late at night, how the maggots tried to crawl out of the clogged sink. A scene I cannot forget.

Chapter 7

Who Is Christian Here?

AROUND FIVE O'CLOCK THE following morning, an officer woke us up screaming. He ordered us to stand and form a line inside the cell. Every morning at 5 a.m., we had to assemble in that same formation before he arrived. The first woman in line was to report if anyone had died during the night.

What a brazen request it was to expect us to report at precisely 5 a.m. since everyone's watch had been confiscated during the initial search and there was no clock in the room. Moreover, there simply was not enough physical space for all nineteen of us to stand at the same time in that tiny cell.

For breakfast, we had a bowl of cold tea and a piece of hard bread. The rest of the day we were given no more food. Around midmorning, the interrogations began. We were told to hold ourselves in readiness. Since the protest started with a Hungarian pastor, I was not surprised that the Hungarian girl was the first to be summoned to interrogation. She likely had never met Pastor Tokes or attended his church, but the poor soul was guilty by ethnic association. Hours passed. The Hungarian girl never returned.

The prison was so overcrowded that the officials decided to release all girls under eighteen so additional adult women could be

Who Is Christian Here?

brought in. When the newcomers arrived in our cell, we gathered around them to find out what was happening on the outside. The women told us how they had been kept all night outside the police station, facedown to the frozen ground as soldiers took turns kicking them with their boots and stepping on their backs.

A young woman lifted her shirt to show us her back. I had never seen such a large hematoma on a person's body. Her flesh was raw from her shoulders down to her hips. She could barely move. These young women were in pain and in desperate need of medical attention.

As to what was happening on the outside, the one thing we had to know was whether the resistance continued, or the protestors had given up. The women confirmed our worst fear. The army received orders to open fire on civilians. The streets were filled with wounded people and dead bodies, for no one dared to help.

As they spoke, fear gripped us, and some of the women went into catatonic shock while others started to wail as for the dead. What if those lying on the sidewalks were our parents, our sisters, brothers, our loved ones? How could unarmed people stand up to tanks and machine guns? It was not a fair fight.

The battle had been lost!

The interrogations continued into late afternoon. One after another, the women returned to the cell the same way: with swollen eyes, blood-red faces, and hair disheveled.

One woman sobbed, "They made me sign a confession to having done something I didn't do. When I refused, they beat me until I signed."

None of the others spoke about what took place in the interrogation room. They just cried. But the rest of us still awaiting our call had a vivid idea what to expect. By that evening, I was the only one not yet interrogated.

That night we slept again sitting up, five women in every bunk bed, resting our heads on one another's shoulders. At 5 a.m., keys rattled the door. We jumped to our feet to form a line, pressing close together, ready to make our report to the officer. He looked in and quickly turned and left.

Breakfast once again was a bowl of cold tea and a piece of stone-hard bread. The morning was quiet except for the random sounds of machine guns going off in the distance. But the silence was short-lived as the cell doors opened, and an officer stood on the other side of the iron bars. We jumped to formation in the narrow space between the bunk beds and the sink. I was close to the back of the line when the officer's question came:

"Who is a Repenter here, Baptist, Pentecostal, or Reformed?"

I couldn't believe it. "Not high school all over again!" I thought.

But what if this was the very moment for which that first day of high school had trained me? What if this was the final exam for which all the previous tests had carefully prepared me? Would I pass it? Would I have the strength to admit that I am guilty of being a Christian—on pain of death this time?

I raised my hand, and for a moment, that motion felt strangely similar to the time I gave my life to Christ. How odd to think that one raising of the hand to follow Jesus would lead to another raising of the hand that would now indict me for following him.

But the officer must not have noticed my raised hand, far back in the line, because he looked as if he was about to leave. Realizing that, I panicked. My biggest fear had always been that I would die having been ashamed of the name of Christ. I didn't want Jesus to deny me before the Father because I was afraid to acknowledge him before men. So, waving my hand, I shouted from the back of the cell, "Here I am. I'm a Repenter! I'm a Baptist!"

The woman standing next to me elbowed me in the ribs. She motioned to put down my hand. Others looked back and whispered under their breath that I was crazy, that I'll get killed. Even the officer seemed a little surprised. Still, he turned around and wrote down my name, the names of my immediate family, and where we lived. When the last cell door was shut, the women felt slightly at ease. I, on the other hand, felt as if I had just signed my death sentence.

Who Is Christian Here?

All morning I thought about the Hungarian girl who never returned. To the officials, she was an obvious culprit because she was Hungarian. But Pastor Tokes was not only Hungarian; he was also a Protestant. Would Protestants be next in this ridiculous manhunt? Will I be next, never to come back? As hours passed, I tried to prepare myself for the interrogation, but the long wait gnawed at my mental strength. What will they ask me? What will I do if they beat me senseless?

Later that afternoon, the cell doors opened. Two officers ordered us to put on our coats and line up outside the cell with our faces to the wall. For a moment, it felt good to be out of that small room, even if we didn't know what to expect.

One by one, the officers turned us around, blinding us with their flashlights and staring us up and down, as if they were looking for someone in particular. I was the first in line, and when I turned, one of the officers exclaimed, "I remember you from our car ride here. Do you remember me?"

"No, sir."

He motioned to turn my face back to the wall.

When the officers finished inspecting each woman, they ordered some to return to the cell and others to follow them. I was among those sent back to the cell. Inside, the room looked hauntingly empty. As we sat in silence, we couldn't help but wonder if we were the "lucky" ones for having remained in prison or if the "lucky" ones were those who had been taken away.

When the heavy doors crashed behind us, a chilling thought crossed my mind: "What if this cell will be my home for the next five years? I would spend the most beautiful years of my life in prison." For the first time since my arrest, I was afraid.

Inside the cell, some women began to weep, facing the walls. Others just stared motionlessly in front of them. The shrieks from the neighboring cells were hair-raising. We could hear them beating dementedly on the doors and walls. In our cell, no one was comforting anyone, and hope was dwindling fast.

From Pain to Purpose

I don't know whether real or recorded, but we could hear screams all around us. Soon, mass hysteria had set in, and one after another, the women succumbed to its icy grip. I could feel my sanity weakening. I needed to talk to God. So, I went to the bathroom behind the busted door and closed my eyes. I needed a word, a feeling, anything that would assure me that God was with me, that I wasn't alone. But no such feelings came.

Can God not see me here? Why is he silent at the time when I need him most? My emotions began spiraling down toward a dark place. Outside the bathroom door, I could hear the women now crying unrestrainedly. In the street, the rattle sound of machine guns going off was impossible to ignore. I looked at the ceiling and whispered:

"Father, I may not feel you right now, but I refuse to believe you have abandoned me. So, if you don't talk to me, I will talk to you, and I will tell you what you told me. You promised that your plans for me are good; that you will never leave me nor forsake me. You promised that you love me with an everlasting love; that you bought me with a price, and I'm yours. You said that you give people for me and nations for my life, and even if I walk through the valley of the shadow of death or fire or high waters, you are with me, and nothing will harm me. Father, I'm scared. All I can do right now is believe that you told the truth. Please, help me."

Back into the cell, some of the women shook uncontrollably. Others wailed, rocking themselves back and forth. It felt as if an evil spirit of fear entered the room and gripped everyone while I was in the bathroom.

I looked at their terrified faces, and for the first time, compassion welled up inside me, as a shepherd would have for his sheep. I knew that I had what these women didn't have—hope beyond this ugly life. I had faith in an eternal life, and a Friend closer to me than the shirt on my body, and I had to tell them about this Friend.

I didn't know how to start, so I blurted, "Does anyone mind if I sing?"

I don't think I could have asked a better question because, in near unison, all the women pleaded, "Please, sing!"

Who Is Christian Here?

I had not planned this, so the first song that came to my mind was "Joyful, Joyful, We Adore Thee," an odd song to sing in a communist prison—the most non-joyful place on earth! But as I sang it, my voice grew louder with the plea, "Melt the clouds of sin and sadness, Drive the dark of doubt away; / Giver of immortal gladness, Fill us with the light of day."[1]

In the dimness of the cell, every word of that song seemed to speak directly to us. The women applauded and asked me to keep singing. I sang every song I could think of, and the songs themselves became witnesses. One song, in particular, was their favorite, and they wanted to learn it. It spoke about that day in heaven when there would be no more pain and no more tears.

We sang together and talked for a long time, and for a few precious moments, we had forgotten that we were prisoners inside a communist prison cell. We could see the guard looking in from time to time, but she never stopped our singing. The women in the other cells also seemed to have quieted down. Even the interrogations ceased while we worshiped. God must have loved our singing so much that he silenced all interruptions!

Soon, the heaviness lifted, and peace settled in our little cell. The women became lively and hopeful, speaking about the day we would all be released. To this day, I attribute that shift in the atmosphere to the power of worshipping God!

The room fell silent, and I thought about what I should do next. I walked to the pile of coats laying on the floor and pulled out my Bible from my coat pocket. When the women saw it, some gasped, others whispered, and many had no idea what it was. But soon, my little Bible traveled from hand to hand. Most of the women had never seen or held a Bible in their hands before. I smiled as I watched them crowding around God's word, all wanting to touch it and take their time reading it. I felt so proud of my little flock. We talked about faith and God until late into the evening. When the light eventually went off, the less crowded beds were a welcomed relief.

---

1. The Romanian lyrics differ slightly, but the message is similar.

From Pain to Purpose

The following day no one came for the 5 a.m. report. We received no breakfast, but none of us seemed to care. Then, about midday, all three doors opened, and a cart full of food was parked in front of our cell. Grilled pork and mashed potatoes with all the trimmings were handed to us, not through a doggy door but served politely, one at a time. We looked at each other confused. What was the meaning of this?

"Is this our final meal or something?" we asked each other under our breath. It didn't matter. We had not eaten for days, and this food smelled delicious.

When we finished our lunch, the guard left open the two outer doors of the cell, and an officer stood in the doorway on the other side of the bars.

"Who wants to go home, and who wants to stay?" he asked, almost smiling.

We looked at him even more confused. No one answered. "What a horrible joke to make," I thought.

But he insisted on knowing whether we wished to go home or stay in prison. Of course, we wanted to go home. What kind of question was that? He assured us that we would all be going home "today." We could hardly believe our ears.

When he left, we could see through the iron bars the women in the cell across the hallway waving at us. We jumped up and down, waving back at them with excitement for the news. That is until we realized that they were not cheering but were trying to get our attention. They waited until the hallway cleared and then shouted, "It's a trap. Don't leave the cell. They are taking us to execute us."

My heart dropped. "That explains the food!"

I went to the back of the cell and closed my eyes.

"May it be done according to Your will."

Chapter 8

Doors No One Can Shut

WE WAITED ALL AFTERNOON for further word about our release, but no one came to free us. One after another, all the other cells emptied except ours. We were left waiting and were not allowed to ask questions of the guards.

Around 10 p.m., our cell doors finally opened. Two prison guards ordered us to follow them into the courtyard. As we left, the patrolling guard in charge of our hallway told us that we were the best cell she had ever had. I think I even spotted a smile on her face.

In the courtyard, the guards led us to a prisoners' truck without windows and told us to climb inside. Some of the women refused and were crying out loud. The guards shoved them in forcefully. I was so exhausted, emotionally, and physically, that I didn't care in the least where they took us.

I was the first to climb into the truck and sat on the floor at the back. Huddling in the pitch dark, we had no clue where we were going. After what seemed like half an hour, the truck stopped. The driver opened the back gate and shouted, "Everybody, out!"

One after another, the women jumped off. Some fell, then took off running. When my turn came, I struggled to jump in my high heels, so the driver reached up to help me.

"Thank you," I whispered.

"Go home, Miss. You're free!" the driver said in a fatherly voice.

I looked around me, but nothing was remotely familiar. There were no streetlights, and I couldn't recognize any landmarks. Most of the women had already scattered in all directions, some hiding in the woods in front of us. "The woods! The Green Forest! I know where I am," I said to myself.

A cellmate who lived near my house asked if she could walk home with me, and we headed together toward some distant lights. Neither one of us said much. I mainly thought about my family. What would they say when they saw me? What would they do to me for putting them through such hell? What if . . . ? No! I refused to think about that.

As we got closer to the lights, we realized that we were near a factory at the edge of the city. We saw some people outside the gate smoking, so we took off running toward them.

"Help us! Please! We were just released from prison. Are the buses still running?"

But the people just stared at us. All prisoners had been freed earlier that day.

"Start walking and watch for a late-night bus that might be going where you are going," a woman finally said.

We walked for nearly an hour and the city looked unrecognizable. Buildings that stood proudly only days before were burned to the ground. Tanks and military vehicles blocked intersections, and frames of incinerated cars littering the asphalt sent the dismal message that this had been a war zone. We plodded on through the rubble, searching for a street we might recognize.

Every so often, we could see a candle flickering in the dark in places where someone had probably died. We walked for almost an hour through this apocalyptic scene and the sight of destruction around me was taking a toll on my mind.

At last, a bus passed, and we flagged it down. We had no money or tickets, but nobody checked. Numbed from head to toe, I found a seat and stared out of the window into the darkness.

Doors No One Can Shut

Flickering candles littered the sidewalks. When it was time for me to step off the bus, I gave my cellmate my Bible. She hid it inside her coat, and we said goodbye.

For the first time since the nightmare began, I was alone and could allow myself to be weak. As I lumbered on toward my apartment, I felt my knees buckling and my sanity slipping away. I wanted to coil on the ground in a fetal position and let my mind escape to a world without violence or pain. But what if I lose my sanity that way? The very thought scared me. I was afraid to let my mind go where it was pulling me. I had to stay in the realm of reality at all costs. So, I kept on repeating aloud, "My name is Lumi. These are my hands. Those are my feet. That is a rock on the ground. I see a light in the distance. The street I am on is . . ." I walked and talked, desperately trying to remain sane.

To my right, I was passing Nuți's apartment. Out of habit, I looked up, and to my surprise, I saw people on her balcony. This seemed strange, being that it was so late at night. I couldn't see, but I hoped that one of those people was Nuți. With all the strength I could muster, I called out her name. She called back. "Lumi, wait, I'm coming down!"

When she saw me, she wrapped her arms around my neck and broke into sobs.

"Where have you been?" she asked.

"I was in prison. Is my family, okay?"

"Yes. But they are worried sick about you."

"Nuți, I'm weak. Help me walk home."

She took a step back and let out a scream:

"My sisters! Mariana and Margareta are dead! Shot in the head by a sniper last Sunday on their way to church."

My knees gave way. I bellowed, "Oh God, no! Please, God! Please, don't let this be true!"

"My father found their bodies at the morgue of the hospital, but the next day he could only find one," Nuți gasped as she spoke.

We clung to each other weeping.

Why? Why?

From Pain to Purpose

Why couldn't life remain the same—with childhood laughter and sled rides? Why prisons, and wars, and death?

We walked together to my house, and when we arrived at the door, I could barely ring the bell. My cousin, who was visiting us from the village, opened the door. When he saw me, his eyes widened, he called my name and ran back inside.

Nuți motioned me to go in, but I didn't have the strength to cross the threshold.

Earlier that day, in the city square, an official announcement was made that all prisoners arrested during the week would be set free by 8 p.m. Ștefan was released sometime in the afternoon and had been calling our house every hour. By midnight he stopped calling. As the hours passed, my parents began to lose hope and assumed the worst.

My sister and brother-in-law lived with us, and I could hear all of them talking in the kitchen. A few minutes later, my brother-in-law came to the door. He, too, said my name and then ran back inside. I could hear him trying to convince my parents that it was really me standing at the door.

"It can't be," I heard my mother say in a raspy voice as if she had been crying for a long time.

She came to the door, and when she saw me, she screamed my name. My father came running behind her, then my sister, followed by everyone else. They all called my name, each trying to hold a part of my body. All I could feel at that moment was massive guilt for having put them through such pain. But we were together again, and that was all that mattered now.

I looked behind me, and Nuți was gone. I could hear her cry down the hollow stairwell.

"Who was that with you?" my mother asked.

Nuți had gone home, never again to taste for herself the sweetness of a family reunion.

My parents looked as if they had aged ten years. Their faces were drawn and swollen, and their eyes were bloodshot red. I felt so guilty for putting them through this ordeal.

From the moment I entered the house, my mother would not let me out of her sight. I could not even go to the bathroom without promising her I would return. Even so, she waited outside the bathroom door. That first night she slept in my bedroom, holding on to my arm.

My father was also visibly shaken up. He confessed that he wanted to strike a bargain with God, that if I came home unharmed, he would become a Repenter. But he felt that a genuine conversion should not be conditional.

"When I become a Repenter," my father said before I went to bed, "it will be because I believe with all my heart." This was the first time my father had ever hinted that he might become a Christian. It was more than I had hoped to hear that night.

The next morning, I heard strange voices outside my bedroom, but I was too tired to open my eyes. When I woke up, my mother told me that visitors had come to see me while I was asleep. The neighbor who lived in the apartment beneath us had heard crying in the middle of the night and thought my parents had received bad news about me. She came to comfort our family.

When my mother told her that I was alive and had come home, the woman didn't believe her. She wanted to see me for herself.

"But the girl is asleep," my mother said.

"I don't care, ma'am. May I please see her?" the woman insisted.

My mother led her to my bedroom, where the woman stood crying at the door. Then she left, and a few minutes later, she returned with her oldest daughter, who also wanted to see me. We rarely spoke with this neighbor, and their sudden interest in what was happening with our family confused my mother.

"Ma'am, may I ask you why you want to see Lumi?" my mother asked.

From Pain to Purpose

"We want to thank her for what she did. You see, we belong to the Hungarian Reformed Church at Maria Station. Laslo Tokes is our pastor. We are a small minority congregation. We could have never protected him alone. Tell Lumi that we will forever be grateful for fighting for our pastor and for us." They all broke down in tears.

"I will," my mother promised.

After I woke up, in the early afternoon, my parents were content just to be with me in the same room. I, on the other hand, was itching to do something, and I knew exactly what I wanted to do.

"Let's go downtown and protest some more!" I blurted.

My parents looked at each other with their mouths hanging open. I could almost hear their thoughts: *You just came from prison for doing that, you stupid child!* But when my father saw that I was serious, he said, "Well, what are we waiting for? Let's all go!"

Every morning when I was in prison, my father reported for work only to tell his boss that he was not staying but was going downtown to the protest.

"Comrade Cristescu, I tell you as a friend that I have strict orders to inform the Party of everyone who is absent," his boss said.

"Chief Comrade, I must tell you that my nineteen-year-old daughter has not been home since the revolution started, and if this government kills children to stay in power, then I . . . am . . . no . . . comrade! Now, if you'll excuse me, I'm going downtown to finish what my daughter started." Every day, my father reported to work on time and then left immediately. And every day, his boss wrote him up.

My father's brother, the staunch communist who was also my boss, phoned our house while I was in prison.

"Brother, please tell Lumi to come to work. The Party is demanding strict account of every employee. If she is not here, they will assume that she is at the protest, and there will be consequences. They want blood!"

"Brother, we don't know where Lumi is. I said some things to her last Saturday, and she hasn't been home since. It's my fault. All of it is my fault."

My uncle was quiet for a moment. "I'll see what I can do. Maybe I can tell them that I gave her the week off."

A few days before my release, the army had refused to follow orders and had stopped firing on civilians. Soldiers and protesters shook hands in the streets as people chanted, "The Army is with us! The Army is with us! Freedom!"

Downtown, all the buildings were covered with anti-communist slogans. People were flying Romanian flags with the communist emblem cut out from the middle. Trucks delivered fresh bread to the protestors, and from the balcony of the opera house, city leaders declared their solidarity with the revolutionaries, proclaiming Timișoara the first free city of Romania.

Next to me, a small boy sitting on his father's shoulders asked in a loud voice, "Daddy, what is freedom?"

Several heads turned.

"Freedom, my son, means that you can have oranges to eat!"

"What are oranges?" the little boy asked.

I looked away to hide my tears. I remembered the last time I ate oranges I was probably his age—before food was scarce—when life was better. I smiled at him, wishing from the bottom of my heart that freedom for him would mean lots and lots of oranges and so much more.

During the protest, a pregnant woman went into labor. Just as the ambulance arrived, she gave birth to a baby girl. The crowd cheered and asked for the infant to be named Victoria. When the parents agreed, one hundred thousand people went ballistic, shouting, "Victory! Victory!" We were one heart and one soul.

One after another, men and women spoke from the balcony of the opera house, encouraging the people. I was chatting with some friends I met in the crowd when suddenly, I heard a familiar voice coming through the intercom: "Our Father who art in heaven, hallowed be Thy Name . . . ."

I looked up and saw Pastor Petrică Dugulescu leading the crowd in the Lord's Prayer. As on command, the people turned their faces toward the cathedral and bowed low to the ground. I knelt with the crowd, weeping that I lived to see this day when a hundred thousand people prayed together in our city square.

For the next ten minutes, the crowd chanted nonstop, "God exists! God exists! God exists!" publicly denouncing forty years of atheism and godless indoctrination. In our little corner of the nation, we knew whom we wanted to serve. But in the capital city, the antichrist still sat on the throne.

When we arrived home, I told my parents that I wanted to go to work the following day. It was the end of the month and the end of the year, and I needed to type the final reports. My parents reluctantly agreed.

When I entered the office, everyone in the room froze as if seeing a ghost. Across from my desk, the dictator's portrait was still hanging on the wall.

"What is *that* still doing there?" I asked, pointing at the picture.

No one answered until Gică, one of the engineers, a tall man, reached up, pulled the picture off the wall, threw it behind a file cabinet, and then did the same with the other two communist symbols.

Everyone was happy to see me, especially Gică. I think he would have drawn horns on the dictator's picture if I had asked him! We talked for a long time, and I finished typing the year-end reports.

Staring out of the dirty window of the tram, I wondered, "Could a country be reborn in a week?" When I arrived home, I saw my family sitting in front of the television. The dictator had just announced a state of emergency, and the people of Bucharest were

Doors No One Can Shut

mandated to gather in Central Square to hear him speak about the events in Timișoara. Romania's one television channel was broadcasting his speech live. We listened from the edge of our seats with our fists clenched. We knew that this could go horribly wrong for our family.

The dictator called the events in Timișoara a coup d'état, which he believed were the treasonous actions of a small group of individuals working with foreign agents to destabilize the sovereignty and integrity of his government. Then, his words became increasingly accusatory. He portrayed the revolutionaries as thieves and hooligans who hated our country and the ideals of communism.

As he spoke, I imagined people in remote parts of Romania watching this, having no idea that a revolution took place in Timișoara. What must they have thought of his speech?

I looked at my mother, and she had that expression on her face that said, *Oh, no, you won't! You will not take my child from me again!*

A neighbor joined us in the TV room. The dictator, voicing his accomplishments, promised to increase the minimum wage, insisting that only communism could continue to bring such prosperity to our nation. It was sad to see how out-of-touch he really was with reality. As he spoke, we heard some people in the crowd shouting. This was highly irregular as everything in communist meetings was tightly monitored to be calm and predictable.

The dictator stopped speaking for a moment as microphones picked up voices rising from the back of the crowd. He resumed, trying to speak over them. But again, he was interrupted. Officials turned on the prerecorded applause to drown out the chatter of the crowd. The dictator stopped again. His wife urged him to continue. He attempted to speak, but he could hear a crescendo of voices booing him. He appeared baffled, which was unusual for a man who was always in control. At that point, secret agents surrounded the dictator and his wife and escorted them from the balcony. The TV station went blank.

From Pain to Purpose

We looked at each other in disbelief. "What does this mean? What is going on in Bucharest? Could it be that the people in the capitol city have joined us and turned against him? Do we have a chance of winning this?"

The TV station abruptly came back on the air. A well-known actor took hold of the camera and the microphone and spoke to the nation.

"The era of lies and terror has ended! Long live free Romania!"

We jumped to our feet. My mother threw open the balcony window and shouted for everyone in the neighboring buildings to hear. "Communism fell! Turn on your TVs. Communism fell!"

Cheers and jubilance flooded the streets as more people found out, and a mass celebration began. I sunk into my chair, trying to believe what I was seeing. We did it! We overthrew communism! Perhaps a nation *can* be reborn in a week!

It was three days before Christmas. Nobody was ready for the holidays, but we had never been more excited to celebrate them.

On December 25, our interim leader addressed the nation on television. He began with a greeting we never heard in the media before. "Merry Christmas!" he said with a smile. Then, his voice turned somber: "The dictators Ceaușescu Nicolae and Elena had been captured, tried, and found guilty of crimes against humanity and genocide. They have been condemned to death . . . and the sentence has been carried out."

My mother fainted in the chair next to me. An image of the dead despots appeared on the television screen. The picture looked gruesome, but it was the closure we desperately needed as a nation. The antichrist was dead. It was Christmas. Christ was born today in Romania!

Chapter 9

Windows in the Heavens

A DEEP SENSE OF peace descended upon the city. Over the next few days, the stores were filled with food, and in homes, the rationing of heat, warm water, and electricity ended. But best of all, hope had returned to our weary souls. Never again would we allow a person to enslave us or a system to rob us of our God-given rights—the freedom to speak up and believe as we desire. This was what we fought and died for. The little boy's question had been answered. This is freedom, the most fragile and costliest of all human rights.

Late at night, we could still hear random gunshots in the streets. We were warned to stay indoors and keep our windows covered. Some said that the dictator's special forces had refused to accept a cease-fire.

Meanwhile, all pictures of the dictator were being removed from schoolbooks, and every communist sign and symbol was coming down from public buildings. Four decades of communism—discarded! Forty years of a system that demonically ruled every aspect of our lives—vanished in one week! Outwardly, everything was changing. But inwardly, how long would it take for the soul of a nation to be truly free?

From Pain to Purpose

Everyone was excited about the new reality. For me, it felt strange to go to church without hindrance and carry my Bible out in the open. Persecution had been part of my life for so long that I didn't know how to be a Christian in freedom. But I had to learn. I wanted to learn. And I loved every moment of it. The words of William Wordsworth rang daily in my ears: "Bliss was in that dawn to be alive, / But to be young was very Heaven!"

I was alive, and I was young, and in a perpetual state of pure celebration. The thought of a future lived in untrammeled freedom made me deliriously happy. I could travel the world and pursue the life I wanted without restrictions and prejudice against my faith. Anything seemed possible! My youthful dreaming knew no bounds. But everything came to a halt a few days later when my father came home with sobering news. He called the family together but spoke directly to me.

"Lumi, I found out that they had sentenced you to death. The list from the penitentiary was released. Your name was on it. On January 4, they planned to make a public example of all of you arrested in the revolution—at the Green Forest."

My father's words hung in the air like razor-sharp icicles. How was I to respond to such news? How does one process such bloodcurdling information?

I whispered to myself: "January 4, 1990, the day of my death!"

But I was not dead. For some unknown reason, God had spared my life. For some unknown reason, I was still here. And what if that reason is not at all unknown? What if the promises God gave me were true? What if, beyond all earthly explanations, there is a purpose for which I *must* live? Suddenly, I felt a great responsibility for being alive, to live a life that had been worth saving.

For the next few months, world evangelists poured into Romania to hold crusades in stadiums and city squares. God was answering our once outrageous prayers to the smallest detail.

Churches joined together to form massive choirs to accompany pastors and preachers in outdoor services. Christian concerts

Windows in the Heavens

and baptismal celebrations took place almost weekly. Church buildings were packed and unable to handle all the spiritually hungry people who had come to hear the gospel, and new congregations were forming. It was as if God opened the windows of heaven and showered us with more blessings than we could contain.

The first free elections in the history of Romania were scheduled for May 20, 1990. Various candidates held their first campaign in Timișoara, which came to be known as the "City of Martyrs."

When the interim leader, who had become a presidential candidate, visited the institute where I worked, I was selected to be part of the welcoming committee to accompany him around the institute and the adjacent factory.

At the end of the tour, someone from his entourage handed me a business card and invited me to attend a private meeting at the hotel where they were staying. Instantly, I knew I had to procure two brand-new Bibles.

I ran to our choir director's house and asked him for two Bibles, one for Romania's future president and the other for the future prime minister. He looked at me suspiciously. It had been only three months since the revolution, and I could tell that he was still hesitant to give out Bibles openly. Fear was ingrained deeply in all of us. Reluctantly, he handed me two new Bibles.

At the hotel, I left the Bibles at the front desk, each containing dedications and the names of their recipients. Not feeling comfortable doing anything more, I prayed that God's Word would not return void. On May 20, the candidates won the elections, becoming Romania's new president and new prime minister.

A few years later, the president said in an interview that the greatest gift he had ever received was a Bible given to him in Timișoara.

From Pain to Purpose

My uncle had quietly retired a couple of months after the revolution, and I continued to work as a secretary. When I was not at work, I was attending a church service somewhere in the city. My energy felt endless, and my heart burned for Bible study and fellowship.

The strong sense of call to ministry reawakened inside me. There was so much optimism in the air, and I was excited to be part of the church's new beginnings in Romania. I could not have guessed that my life was about to take an entirely different turn.

It was a beautiful early summer day. Our church had planned a baptismal service at the river outside the city. No longer in hiding, we could express our faith openly. People traveled by cars, vans, and buses to celebrate the historic event. I took a taxi from the city to the baptismal site.

There was incredible jubilation as our choir sang, and the new believers, dressed in white, stepped into the river to profess their faith. There could not have been a more perfect scene to remind us that Christ always wins in the end.

About midway through the service, a burgundy-colored van pulled up and parked near us on the grass. Two men hopped out and walked in our direction.

"This service could not get any better" I thought, when I recognized one of them to be Pastor Petrică Dugulescu.

Since the day I gave my life to Christ, in my estimation, no one had surpassed his preaching. I knew we would be in for a treat. But, as the service drew to a close, Pastor Petrică never took the microphone. And I started to wonder just why he had come.

Small groups of people lingered in conversation before heading off to their cars. Ștefan and I stayed behind chatting with some friends, when someone interrupted to say that Pastor Petrică was looking for us. Glancing at Ștefan, I shrugged.

When Pastor Petrică saw us, he greeted us with his signature warm smile and then introduced us to the man standing next to him.

Windows in the Heavens

"Please, meet the dean of the psychology department at Tennessee Temple University in America."

Then, he continued:

"I want both of you to take an English test today. There are scholarships available for you to study in America at this Christian university."

I felt instantly dizzy. I never told Pastor Petrică about my prayers. Yet, this could not be a coincidence. But why now when there is so much to do in Romania? For five years I prayed for this moment to come, and now I felt unsure. Romania needed me. But studying the Bible in America was all I've ever wanted. It was my life's dream, my true north every time I lost hope. My thoughts ran unbridled. What if my English is not good enough to pass the exam? What if I fail and embarrass myself? What if I'm just dreaming right now?

At Pastor Petrică's church, over two dozen young people, from all over the country, all as nervous as I was, were waiting to take the test. The results would be announced by telephone that afternoon. All I could think of was, "Could this be the answer to my impossible prayer?"

At home, around 3 p.m., the phone rang.

"Lumi, congratulations! You passed! We will be in touch with you about the visa and the other documents you will need," a young man said.

"What about Ștefan?" I asked.

"I'm sorry, your boyfriend didn't pass."

I ran into the kitchen to tell my parents.

"I passed! I passed! I'm going to America!"

My father looked at me disdainfully:

"Be serious, girl. Who is going to send *you* to America? I wish that priest of yours stopped raising young people's hopes like this."

But I refused to indulge my father's pessimism. I went to my room and fell to my knees.

"Father, I don't even know what to say. I can't believe you are doing this for me. I can't believe you answered my crazy impossible prayer. But now I know that nothing is impossible with you. Thank you."

The doorbell rang. Ștefan's face hid behind a bouquet of long-stem, brightly colored gladiolas.

"Congratulations, Miss America!" he said, kissing me on both cheeks. My parents smiled. They liked Ștefan and were already treating him like family.

The news was beginning to sink in, but that night I couldn't sleep. The thought of leaving the only country I ever knew overwhelmed me. The very idea that God had choreographed the fate of a nation to answer the prayer of a teenage girl was borderline fantasy. If this was true, there was nothing that I couldn't do with God!

It was July, and I would soon have to go to Bucharest for my visa. I begged my parents to postpone their three-week vacation so we could spend more time together before I left. But my father's response was always the same. "Stop talking crazy! Who will send *you* to America?" They packed their suitcases and left.

That week I turned in my notice at work and took the train to the village to say goodbye to my grandmother. As the train pulled into the station, I felt a deep sense of loss in the pit of my stomach. Looming over the houses was the Burzău Hill I used to climb with other kids to steal grapes from the government's vineyard. To my right was the Criș riverbank, where I meandered day in and day out, minding my relatives' cows, losing sight of them most of the time because I couldn't stop playing. I loved that little village with its quirky people and blessed traditions that made my childhood so happy.

I walked slowly along the dusty road from the train station to my grandmother's house, letting every memory seep deep into my soul. When the New World with its slick roads and skyscrapers will try to woo my heart away I wanted no rival to the beauty of this little village.

From a distance, I could see my grandmother sitting on the bench outside her house. I waved at her, and when she saw me, I

Windows in the Heavens

could see her wiping her tears. She was frailer than when I had last seen her. I kissed her on both cheeks, and we sat on the bench, holding hands.

"My dear Lucica[1], only the Lord knows how much I prayed for you when I heard that you were in prison," she said, wiping her big, brown eyes.

I kissed her hands.

"Thank you. The Lord heard your prayers. I'm here now."

"Yes, but what is this I hear, that you are going to America?"

"Măicuța, that's why I'm here. I will be leaving in a few weeks, but I wanted to see you before I left."

Her eyes filled with tears again.

"America is so far. You will be among foreigners. But the Lord will be with you."

She searched for her handkerchief, and I kissed her wet cheek.

"I can't stay long. I'm taking the next train back to Timișoara, but I will see you next summer, yes?"

"I don't think we will see each other again on this earth," Măicuța said.

"Of course, we will." But in my heart, I knew she was right.

I waved for a long time until I could no longer see her. When I turned the corner, I burst into tears and ran back to hug her one more time. A neighbor saw me crying as I passed her house. "Weep, my girl, weep, because you won't see your Măicuța again," the woman said. I ran the entire way to the station, so no one else would stop me or see me crying.

My mind raced as I settled into my compartment. Life is like a train ride. Each new station is a new chapter we are writing, and each station we leave behind is a chapter that has ended and would never be rewritten. Moving forward means leaving something behind. I couldn't hold onto my childhood forever, to my little village, to Măicuța. I was racing toward the future, and I loved it and hated it all the same.

---

1. The name by which my grandmother called me.

From Pain to Purpose

I returned to Timișoara, and the following day was Cristian's wedding. I dreaded it, but Ștefan was eager to go, probably to make sure that Cristian didn't back out. The dress I wore was a bit flashy for the occasion, but I hoped it would mask the emotional rollercoaster I was feeling inside. The service dragged on. But when the bride and groom knelt at the altar for the exchange of vows, eyebrows lifted.

Pastor Petrică laid hands on them and asked the groom the customary question: "Cristian, out of love and your own free will, do you take this woman to be your wife?"

"Yes," Cristian said.

Knowing that Cristian and I had dated for several years until recently, Pastor Petrică looked over the crowd in my direction. As he did, others followed his gaze, and momentary chatter erupted.

"Cristian," he reiterated, "please look at me. Do you vow before God that out of love, and unforced by circumstances, you take this woman to be your lawful wife?"

"I do."

The wedding celebration began, and when Ștefan and I were ready to leave, we kissed the bride and the groom and handed them the customary monetary gift.

In the courtyard, I let out a sigh of relief, glad that it was over. But, as we walked toward the gate, I heard someone call my name. Behind us, Cristian stood in the doorway. Our eyes locked. The pleading stare on his face put a lump in my throat. It was as if saying, "Even now . . . if you want to . . ." We stared at each other motionless and irreparably apart until I felt a tug at my hand.

"Let's go," Ștefan said.

For my twentieth birthday, Ștefan planned to surprise me with a trip to Switzerland where his mother's side of the family lived. But since plans had changed, he bought my plane ticket to America instead.

A few days later, I picked up my passport, which strangely, still carried the name of the Socialist Republic of Romania. I smiled. So long as it was a legal document, I couldn't care less that it called for proletarians of all countries to unite. I had a passport in my hands!

Pastor Petrică rented a minibus for us to go to Bucharest to get our visas, and when my parents returned from their vacation, I had already packed my suitcases.

My father stared speechless at the American visa inside my passport. My mother just cried. I was to leave Romania in four days' time—one week after I turned twenty and eight months to the day after the revolution.

I spend those last four days visiting relatives in the city to say goodbye. They were the same relatives who had once told me that I had no future because I became a Repenter. I graciously hugged them and wished them well. They seemed happy for me. Whenever anyone asked what I would be studying abroad, my answer was always: "The Bible!"

On my last night in Romania, my mother slept in my room, holding on to my arm. But this time, it was not a mad dictator who threatened to take me away, but the very freedom for which we fought. On the morning of my flight, my parents cried almost nonstop, trying to find the strength to let go of me a second time.

The small airport felt like a funeral home. In the distance, the only airplane on the runway was the "tomb" in which I would willingly enter, to be resurrected anew into a different world.

As I reached for the last door before the checkpoint, I waved at my family and the friends who had come to see me off. Ștefan pulled me back and held my face in his hands.

"I love you, Lumi. Remember this."

He pressed his lips onto mine and then held me tight to his chest. I pulled back, feeling awkward doing that in front of my parents. But more surprising than the awkwardness of that moment was the realization that I couldn't return Ștefan's love. Not the way he wanted it, not the way he deserved.

From Pain to Purpose

Through the small window of the plane, I could see my family still hanging on to the wire fence, looking up. There was not one cloud in the sky, and a new chapter was about to begin.

Chapter 10

No "Cats" in America

THE PAN AMERICAN JUMBO jet glided effortlessly over the Atlantic Ocean.

"So, what will you study in college?" the young man seated next to me asked, passing the time.

"The Bible," I answered, excited that I understood his question.

He glanced at me, and with a slight jeer in his voice, he said, "You will change your mind. You'll see. America changes people." His words took me by surprise. I thought everybody in America was a Christian.

As the plane hovered over the New York skyline, I said almost audibly, "This is insane! I'm really here!"

When the airplane touched down on American soil, I breathed deeply for the first time in eight months. I was far from revolutions, far from political unrest, and senseless killings. No one could harm me here. And I instantly loved this country.

For the first few days in America, I woke up in the middle of the night in an absolute panic, certain that the whole thing was a dream. Drenched in sweat, I feared that I was not actually in America, not really at a Christian university, and by no means free.

From Pain to Purpose

Every morning, before I was fully awake, I touched the walls next to my bed to make sure I wasn't dreaming. Then, I'd let my mind wander, thinking about my future in this new country. Would I like it here? Would Americans like me? How might God fulfill his promises to me here?

Excited about the future, I felt blessed to have received this scholarship. As for the other twenty-two Romanians who came with me, perhaps their access to this blessing came purely from knowing the right people, or from being the right persons' children. For still others, maybe it was a simple stroke of luck to have been at the right place at the right time.

But for me, this scholarship represented God's gift for all the pain I endured, for having turned the other cheek, and for not denying him on pain of death. This presidential scholarship was the launching pad from which God would propel me into the ministry. It was the cherry on top of every answered prayer I had ever received. And yet, sometimes, late at night, when my thoughts roamed back to Romania, I felt a large knot in the back of my throat.

Before the semester began, I met with my advisor to choose an academic major. In my broken English, I told him, "I want to preach. So, I choose Pastoral Studies major."

"Oh, no! You don't understand," he said. "Only men can study that." Then, he quickly pointed to other majors that I could consider.

"Then I will take Missions major to be a missionary."

A Romanian couple working with Precept Ministries became our adoptive parents. They often invited all twenty-three of us to their home on weekends, where we played Super Mario and ate Romanian food. It was a welcomed change after being cooped up all week on campus under a myriad of strict rules.

On many occasions, when American peculiarities stumped us, our adoptive parents deciphered them for us. Then we would

No "Cats" in America

laugh realizing how different the two cultures were and how much we still had to learn.

But the best part was that this couple came on campus once a week in the evening to teach Inductive Bible Studies in Romanian. I loved how God made the desire of my heart to study the Bible come to pass so perfectly.

The first letter that I received from home was from Ștefan. It was a love letter written with tenderness and longing. I loathed that I didn't feel the same way about him, and it was time to be honest about it. Fortunately, the distance made it easier to break off the relationship.

A few days later, a letter from my family arrived. Outside the post office, I ripped open the homemade envelope. My parents, sister, and brother-in-law each wrote several pages of heartfelt words, but my father's letter, especially, took me by surprise.

"Dear Lumi, I tell all my friends and coworkers that you are at university in America. Please tell me exactly what you study so I can tell them. I'm proud of you."

As I read the letter, mixed emotions churned within me. My father was no longer ashamed of me! That was good. But deep inside, I couldn't shake the memory of his hurtful words spoken to me only a few short months before. I couldn't stop thinking that he had done nothing to make my scholarship possible. He didn't encourage me through the process, nor had he ever believed in me. Since I became a Christian, he only reminded me how I failed to measure up to his expectations.

But ultimately, I told myself, once again, that his actions were the result of his unredeemed nature. So, in my next letter, I told him just how happy I was to do what I had always wanted—study theology.

On my way back to my dorm, I tried to imagine what it must have been like for my parents when they realized that I was, indeed, going to America. I remembered how they used to tell me that I would be lucky in life because, as a little girl, I fell in the outhouse.

From Pain to Purpose

At that time, I was trying to win a dare with my older cousin. As I lowered myself through the hole of the outhouse seat, I missed the slippery rock underneath it and fell knee-deep in feces. According to some Romanian folklore, that good soaking would bring me good luck. I never understood the connection, but my parents always laughed when they remembered that story. Even now, I was almost certain that they were attributing my "good fortune" in coming to America to that outhouse incident in the village, rather than to God who answered my prayers. Either way, the memory brought a smile to my face.

Early in the fall, the university organized a tour of Washington, DC, for the Romanian students to show us the sites and teach us some American history at the same time. We were spellbound by the beauty of this nation, its blessed past, and the gracious people who opened their homes to us. The smallest things about America fascinated me, especially holiday celebrations and meals.

When my American roommate heard that I knew nothing about Halloween, she insisted that I visit a haunted house with other students from campus. The experience terrified me. Coming from a country that openly practiced witchcraft in many forms, I couldn't understand why American Christians considered a haunted house to be a place of entertainment. Nonetheless, I was intrigued. Every fresh experience helped me better understand this new culture.

The following month, a wealthy family invited all the Romanian students to celebrate our first Thanksgiving at their country estate. The hosts were friends of the Romanian missionary couple and were terrific believers. Yet, coming as I did from a communist country, the expression "wealthy Christians" was an oxymoron. I didn't know that such persons existed. I thought it impossible for anyone, but especially for Christians, to own so much private property. It was not a judgmental commentary, just a simple observation. This novelty challenged my existing mindset, but I was eager to learn.

No "Cats" in America

At Christmastime that year, the same couple invited us back to their estate. Despite their earthly affluence, I got to know them less as "rich Christians" and more as persons of authentic faith I wished to imitate. God was reshaping my understanding of the world and of his church.

Although we didn't all know each other before we came to America, our group of twenty-three Romanians became quite a choral ensemble. We visited several churches to sing and share our testimonies of faith and raise financial support for the college.

On a Sunday we traveled to a large church in a Nashville suburb. I had never previously shared my testimony in public since I thought I couldn't express myself coherently enough in English. Also, I didn't think my story was so unusual. Most Romanian Christians have gone through much more difficult experiences. But most of all, I hadn't yet processed all the events that had happened to me, especially those surrounding my imprisonment, and I wasn't ready to talk about it.

The pastor introduced us and told the congregation that two young people in our group had spent time in prison under the communist regime. He invited us onto the stage and handed me the microphone to share my story first. I don't believe it crossed the pastor's mind that some of us might not yet have a good handle on the English language, being that we had just arrived in the country, nor was I told beforehand that I would have to share my testimony in that church.

I took the microphone and stared blankly in front of me. Several hundred people looked uncomfortably in my direction, waiting for me to say anything. The pastor squirmed in his seat, and a Romanian stepped forward and offered to interpret for me.

"Just say something," my friends whispered from their seats. But I could not say one word in English or Romanian. I stared at the crowd and felt like passing out. Someone helped me off the stage and I sat in my chair, wishing that I could find a hole in the ground to hide in forever. "Maybe public speaking will not be my future calling," I muttered to myself.

Before the end of our first semester, Pastor Petrică had already visited us once at school. As our spiritual father, he looked out for us and spent time privately with each one of us to see how we were really doing. Before we left Romania, he taught us as much as he knew about America, but nothing could have prepared us fully for this new and complicated world.

My biggest struggle remained the language. My English improved during the first few months in America, but not enough to understand the thick Southern accent of the people around me, including my professors. Additionally, I couldn't understand the archaic wording of the King James Version of the Bible that the school expected us to read. Most sermons and lectures sounded like gibberish.

I also struggled with the fact that all chapel and church services were mandatory. If we missed as many as three, we were instantly "campused." This meant that we were confined to our dorm room for an entire weekend, as to a prison. We were allowed to go only to the dining hall for a limited time, and no other interactions, including phone calls, were permitted.

If we were late for church or chapel or left the service early, we were also penalized. To work off our demerits, we had to clean toilets for a week or perform other menial jobs around campus. If we accumulated a certain number of demerits, we could be expelled from school. This baffled me. Less than a year earlier, I risked my life to go to church. And now I was being forced to attend, or else risk being thrown out of college. Really, now?

I was confused and often walked alone around campus trying to make sense of it all. I felt decidedly alone and didn't understand why God brought me to this school. I missed my friends back home, my little church, and our way of life. Everything here in America seemed different—not wrong, just different.

No "Cats" in America

But I pressed on, convinced that I could learn the language better and feel more at home if I made more American friends. So, at mealtimes, I often sat with Americans in the dining hall and made small talk with my American roommate, despite how busy she always reminded me that she was.

One day at lunch, a Romanian friend told me that one of his American buddies had asked about me.

"I am not interested unless he is studying to be a pastor," I said emphatically.

I knew that God had called me to preach. But after being told so many times, in Romania and America, that I was not allowed to preach as a woman, I was convinced that I had misunderstood God. So, I resigned to the idea that God likely meant for me to become, not a pastor, but a pastor's wife.

My friend knew very little about his American buddy, but he thought I should at least give him a chance.

The next day, I sat with my Romanian friends in the dining hall, and a young American asked if he could join us at our table. When he left to get a drink, my friend hinted that this was his buddy who had asked to meet me.

He was handsome and confident, and his smile brightened the room. When he returned to the table, I couldn't eat another bite. My whole body shook. My friend introduced us, and I immediately asked, "So, Damon, what is your major?"

"Pastoral Studies," he answered with a big smile.

When those two words came out of his mouth, I couldn't breathe. My friend winked at me, and I knew, beyond any doubt, that I was staring my fate in the face.

Damon was intelligent and funny and was intrigued by my Romanian culture. We spent a lot of time together, and in a relatively short period, my English improved exponentially. As weeks and months passed, I was falling in love with Damon, and whenever I thought of him, I imagined the next Billy Graham preaching to the masses, and me as his biggest intercessor. I couldn't wait to hear more about Damon's call to ministry, his plans as a future pastor, and how God had been working all along in his life. I wanted to have devotions with him every morning at school and grow in our faith together.

We soon began to date exclusively and walked for hours around campus, sharing stories about our lives. But my heart broke as I listened to Damon talk of his childhood in a home filled with pain and abuse, followed by ten years in an institutional home for boys after his parents divorced. He had no relationship with his parents and didn't know for sure the whereabouts of his eleven siblings. Behind that bright smile hid a troubled young man, and I felt immense sadness for him.

"I don't need my family," Damon said one day. "They abandoned me in an orphanage. Why should I so much as even look for them?"

I had just received word that Măicuța had died, and I was grieving.

"We all need family. You should at least try to reconnect with some of your siblings," I said.

A few months later, he did just that, and his father and one of his sisters visited him at the college. Damon was exuberant.

A year had passed since I came to America, and I was now a sophomore, studying to be a missionary. Yet, for some reason, I felt spiritually dry and unsettled. The school had begun to show signs of monetary distress, and all the Romanian students received weekly letters requesting that we look for financial sponsors. Our scholarships had become a burden that the school could no longer sustain.

Moreover, the strict rules by which we had to abide made me feel like I was a kindergartener. The inability to leave the campus constrained me as though I were a prisoner. I not only missed my family, but I missed the freedom to roam about the city and go wherever I wanted. The lack of privacy in my dorm room also cut into my prayer life and intimacy with God. The language barrier made theology a subject I no longer enjoyed. But most of all, I

No "Cats" in America

became unsure about my future. Somehow, I lost my sense of calling and desire to be in the ministry. I questioned whether I wanted to return to Romania when I graduated. And if so, what would I do there? What about Damon? I desperately needed guidance. I lacked direction for my life and had no one to talk to about it. Even God, who always gave me answers, seemed strangely far away.

I struggled to maintain a sense of satisfaction, and I thought that a change in my major might bring me the fulfillment I craved. A couple of months into my second year, I planned to change my track from missions to a nursing major. But there was something else I also needed to do. I needed to break off my relationship with Damon. After a year of dating, I had serious questions about his spiritual maturity, relationship with God, and his fitness for ministry. Overall, I just wanted a fresh start.

Damon was renting a room in a house owned by his friend. Since the school frowned upon students going to movie theaters, Damon picked me up from campus to watch a film at his house. The entire day I rehearsed just how I would tell him that I wanted us to part ways.

We went into the living room to be alone, but before I could speak a word, from behind the couch, Damon pulled out a bouquet of roses.

"Lumi, will you marry me?"

Chapter 11

Prison without Walls

I stared at Damon in disbelief. Seeing my hesitation, he added, "Lumi, we are good for each other. We should get married."

This was not how I wanted the evening to go. I had prepared my break-up speech, but instead of giving it, I threw my arms around Damon's neck and said, "Yes, I will," while inside, I hated myself for not carrying through with my plan. He slipped a small diamond ring on my finger, and I returned to my dorm that night as an engaged-to-be-married woman.

It had been a year and a half since I had come to America. Although my English had improved, I was still a million miles from understanding the American culture and all the subtleties of a foreign mindset. Beyond wanting to be in ministry with my husband, I had no further plans. As for marriage, I had no idea how couples in America lived their lives together. American customs were different, but I relied on Damon to teach me, and he seemed more than happy to do so. The joy of being a pastor's wife dispelled all the doubts I had previously held about my now fiancé, and I was excited to marry him.

It was Damon's last semester of college, and he undertook a pastoral internship, teaching the youth group of a church in town.

Prison without Walls

I was excited to see him immersed in ministry. He was not the most gifted teacher, but I believed that God would use him mightily in time.

During the long hours we spent on the phone in the evenings, Damon continued to disclose deeper hurts from his past. I wanted to relate to him, but I couldn't. Our stories could not have been more different. I thought of sharing my concerns with others, but I knew they would counsel me to break up with him. His emotional baggage was insurmountable.

When Damon came on campus for church or chapel services, he had a new habit of criticizing every sermon we heard, insisting that his understanding of the Greek text was so much better than that of the preachers. His arrogance was unsettling to me.

Even his closest friends noticed the vulgar language he'd picked up and the change in his attitude, and they spoke with him about it. When he ridiculed their concerns, they distanced themselves from him, even though they had been his friends since the first day of college and were about to graduate together in a few months. As his fiancée, I saw this rift with his friends as my chance to show him undying devotion, even though inside, my own doubts about marrying him were mounting.

One of my Romanian friends was particularly vocal about my not marrying Damon, at least not so soon. But I refused to listen to her and eventually stopped talking to her altogether. In my mind, an engagement was as serious as marriage. Besides, Damon was about to become a pastor, and I was about to become a pastor's wife. I let nothing and no one cloud my thinking.

One evening, Damon called to tell me that he wanted our wedding to be on his May graduation day. I had hoped for a different time and a different place. Since he didn't have a strong relationship with his family, I wanted us to go to Romania. There, he could meet my family, ask my father for my hand in marriage and have the wedding ceremony in my home church.

"I hope you realize that this wedding is not about you," Damon said to me one evening on the phone. "I talked to my parents

From Pain to Purpose

and some of my siblings, and they all want to come to the wedding. This wedding will be a family reunion for us. Isn't that exciting?"

I didn't have the heart to tell him how much it bothered me that his family was his sole focus on our wedding day, and I felt selfish to have considered our wedding to be about me. Besides, neither one of us had the money to travel overseas. So, we proceeded along with Damon's plans.

A month before the wedding, Damon bought me a secondhand, off-white wedding dress, insisting that I wear it. While it looked cute on me, I preferred a pure white dress since I was a virgin. In my culture, the symbolism of the white dress was important for a bride. Damon could not understand what the big deal was.

The office manager where I worked on campus noticed my distress. She took me to the mall and bought me a white wedding dress. A few days later, Damon and I went to the justice of the peace as two of his friends witnessed our wedding vows.

On the morning of Damon's graduation day, I was taken violently ill. That afternoon, an unlicensed minister officiated our religious ceremony, which took place on the grounds of the Chattanooga Choo-Choo. It was a far cry from the church wedding I had dreamed of as a young girl. But at this point, I was willing to do just about anything to be married to the next greatest world evangelist.

Our marriage, however, had a solemn footnote. The college's policy stipulated that my scholarship was available to me only if I remained single. If I were to marry before graduating, then I would automatically lose the grant. But to me, Damon's calling to be a pastor and my calling to be a pastor's wife were infinitely more important than any financial assistance or scholarship. So, after two years of college, without giving it a second thought, I walked away from my full-ride presidential scholarship.

Along the way to our Florida honeymoon, we visited some of Damon's long-lost siblings. In Florida, we stayed with his sister and her family in a small two-bedroom apartment. She and her husband gave us their master bedroom, while they slept with their two-year-old son in a single bed.

Each night I went to sleep alone while Damon and his sister enjoyed catching up. When I said something to him about it, Damon reminded me that this was the first time he had seen his family since he was a kid and that it was selfish of me to deprive him of the joy.

We returned home to Tennessee on a Saturday night, and I could hardly wait to go to church the following day. I wanted to start our marriage on the right foot. But equally exciting to me was to go to church because I wanted to, not because I had to, as in college.

With our suitcases from the honeymoon lying open on the floor, our tiny apartment looked even smaller and untidy. The next day, I woke up early and sat on the edge of the bed with my feet dangling down the two mattresses we stacked together in a corner.

"I'll go and get ready," I said as I got up.

Suddenly my body thrust violently forward.

Instinctively, I looked at Damon. His fist was still clenched.

"I don't want to go to church. Can't you understand?" he hollered.

I stared at him in shock. I couldn't even cry. My back burned from the force of his punch.

Back in bed, I turned my face to the wall and repeated in my mind over and over again: "What just happened *never* happened!"

The rest of the day was a blur.

I woke up early the following morning to iron Damon's shirt for his work as a restaurant waiter. As I watched his car disappear around the corner, I said to myself, "One day, that man will be a pastor, and everything will be perfect."

Staring into the distance, with my head pressed against the window frame, I wanted more than anything in the world to be the wife of an American pastor. I knew dozens of Romanian girls who would have killed to be in my shoes. "I'm happy," I said out loud

From Pain to Purpose

as if trying to convince myself. But my body protested. I began to shake and gasp for air, and the walls around me started closing in like a prison. I grabbed my face with both hands and screamed, "What have I done? God, what have I done?" And I could almost hear Satan's maniacal laughter, "You just ruined your life!"

Every day when Damon came home from work, I was as cheerful and loving as I could be. Yet nothing I did seemed to make him happy. I was already a good cook, but I taught myself how to prepare American dishes, hoping these would make Damon feel loved.

Daily, I cleaned the house and washed clothes by hand in the bathtub. Yet barely a day passed without hearing him say, "You are a millstone around my neck. You live in *my* country, eat *my* food, and stay in *my* house."

Sometimes, before he went to work, he checked the top of the doorposts for dust. If they were not cleaned when he returned, I could expect to be beaten.

We didn't own a television for the first two years of our marriage, but I was content to listen to music on a clock radio that someone at college had given me.

"This radio uses too much electricity!" Damon shouted one day, yanking the plug out of the wall.

At that point, I was still on a student visa, and I couldn't legally work in America. I didn't have a driver's license and had no friends. The clock radio was my only connection to the outside world. But I was taught to be submissive to my husband, so I stopped listening to the radio.

At night, Damon forbade me to come near the middle of the bed. One day he drew an imaginary line for me down the center of the mattress and said that I was never to cross it. But in my sleep, sometimes I would do it, and next I knew, I would find myself violently kicked out of bed.

One night, after another line-crossing, I gathered myself up from the floor and went to sleep on the couch in the living room. Damon followed behind me, taking away all pillows, blankets, and coats from the closet that I might use to keep myself warm. Before he went back to bed, he reminded me how lucky I was because he didn't believe in divorce. Then he added, "So I pray every day that you die!"

I lifted the large seat cushions from the couch and spent the night curled up underneath them, trying to keep warm.

Two years into our marriage, I lived in debilitating fear of Damon during the day and in terror of him at night. There was no predictability to his angry outbursts and no predictability when he might take out his anger specifically on me. I was in a constant state of anxiety, but I learned quickly to hide my bruises and conceal all pain.

From the outside, Damon and I looked like the most loving couple anyone would know. In public, I played along, laughed, put on a mask, and never showed a hint of unhappiness. When we met with Damon's friends, he was the life of the party. Everybody wanted to be around him. No one would have believed me if I had told them that he beat me at home.

Damon liked the fact that I hid the abuse. He considered it my duty, as a submissive wife, to make him always look good in front of others. I, on the other hand, was ashamed and afraid to talk to anyone about the beatings. I was ashamed because I had failed to marry a godly man, which was a negative reflection on my ability to hear from God. I should have prayed and fasted more. And I was afraid to tell anyone because I didn't know what he would do to me if I disclosed the abuse. I also didn't believe any marriage could ever recover if something like that were to be made public. But above all, I believed Damon would change, and I didn't want his past to mar his future image as a minister of the gospel. Somehow, it all made sense to me at that time. But the cycle of abuse continued, going from rising tension, to beating, to regret, to momentary peace, until it started all over again.

I was the perfect victim. I was meek and naive and had no family to protect me in this country. I was isolated from my friends and without a church family. I was entirely at his mercy.

From Pain to Purpose

"America is a dangerous place," Damon often reminded me. "You could get killed just checking the mail."

We lived in a suburban triplex on top of a scenic ridge. It was doubtful that I would be in any danger while checking the mail. But in America, I had only lived on a closed campus at a small Christian university. Damon's eyes were the only window through which I saw the rest of this country. Whatever he told me, I believed.

"Trust me. I'm your protector. You don't know this country as I do," he often said.

Deep in my heart, I wanted to believe that Damon was my protector, but I couldn't help feeling that he was my jailer.

Despite everything, I held on to the hope that Damon would soon become a pastor, and we would go to church, and everything would be better. But he must have suspected that I was clinging to that hope because, one day, out of the blue, he said, "Just so you know, I never wanted to be a pastor. That was just a phase I was going through in college, and I didn't want to change my major and lose all my credits."

I was devastated! His words squashed the last glimpse of hope I had clung to. I forfeited my life's dream because I thought he would be a pastor! I had lost my presidential scholarship because I believed more in his call than I believed in my own! I squandered God's gift to me, and the only thing that Damon said was, "Tough luck! Deal with it! That's life!"

His confession broke me mentally, physically, and spiritually. I couldn't pray anymore and had no one to talk to about it. I felt betrayed, forsaken by God, and trapped in a marriage with no way out. Worst of all, I could see in Damon's eyes that my brokenness made him feel all the more powerful.

Prison without Walls

One day Damon came home from work angry. I had just finished preparing dinner and had baked a blackberry pie from scratch, one of his favorites, still warm from the oven. When I told him that dinner was ready, he walked into the kitchen, grabbed the pie, and threw it into the trash can.

"This is what I think of you and your pie," he shouted.

There had been no argument beforehand to trigger his outburst, and I had no idea how to help him. I didn't want him to see me crying, so I left the kitchen. He followed me into the living room. Then, without warning, he slugged me in the back, and I fell to the floor.

For the first time in my life, I thought of myself as worthless and unloved, even by God. I laid with my face on the ground, my tears rolling between the cracks of the aged hardwood. I was so ashamed of my life that I prayed a prayer I never thought I would: "Father, please look away. I don't want you to see me like this."

I limped to the bathroom to wash my face and looked at myself in the mirror. How did I get here? How did I get under this man's feet? All I wanted was to serve God.

Damon came to the bathroom door with an apology.

"I'm sorry I hit you, but I hope you realize that I do it out of mercy because divorce is a sin. I don't want to throw you out into the street as you deserve."

I didn't know what I could possibly have done to deserve being thrown into the street. But then, one day, Damon told me.

"What bothers me about you, is that you don't praise me enough as a wife should. You don't appreciate my superior intellect and good looks and my god-like qualities."

Then, pausing for a moment, he declared, "I *am* a god!"

I stared at him in shock. His words sounded freakishly familiar. What were the odds that two men, with the same delusions of grandeur, could have ended up in my life?

By this time, I had applied for a work permit, and when I received it, Damon made sure that I worked at the same restaurant as he. I still didn't drive, and we were not permitted to work the same shift since it posed a conflict of interest. So, Damon drove me to work and back each day, but after a while, he stopped picking me up, and I had to ask coworkers for rides home.

I would leave pleading messages for Damon on the answering machine until somebody eventually felt sorry for me and drove me home. When I stepped into the house, Damon was either asleep, pretending to be sleeping, or laughing at me.

Sometimes, when I checked the mail or took the trash out, Damon would lock me out of the house and refuse to let me in for hours at a time. He said it was "to teach me a lesson." The only lesson I learned was that he was in control of my life and that I was not. His intentional and systematic abuse gave him a warped sense of power.

I was content with my job as a restaurant hostess, but what I really wanted was to finish my college education. I begged Damon to let me enroll in a public university to continue my nursing studies. He said that if I wanted to go to college, I would have to take the bus to school and pay for my classes from my own earnings.

I rode the city bus downtown several days a week for the next two years, taking one or two courses each semester. Eventually, I learned to drive and went to school full-time while working on the weekends. The first time I drove alone was to nursing school, almost an hour away. That evening, when I arrived home, Damon looked surprised to see me. "I was so sure that you would die in a car crash today," he said laughing.

During my last year of nursing school, my father wrote me a letter. He had applied for an American visa and planned to stay with us for six months. The timing was terrible for many reasons. But culturally, I couldn't refuse my father's visit.

Earlier that year, my father had become a Christian. His radical conversion had stunned everyone who knew him, including his siblings. When he shared his testimony, he shocked the congregation when he described in detail his plan to kill my sister and me on the day Dorina got baptized, eight years earlier.

When my father became a Repenter, he was instantly delivered of his alcohol addiction, smoking, and cursing, and he stopped beating my mother. He was a brand-new person and wanted me to see how Christ had changed his life.

By the time my father arrived, I had learned to cover up my pain so convincingly that he could detect nothing but happiness after living in the same house with us for six months!

One day, when my father was still with us, Damon came home angry. He wanted to take me to the bathroom to slap me. I begged him not to beat me with my father in the house.

"You can beat me as much as you want after my father leaves," I negotiated with him in the bathroom.

I became so accustomed to Damon's abuse that I was now giving him permission to beat me. I became someone I could not even recognize.

My father returned to Romania before I graduated from nursing school, and that fall, I began work as a nurse at a family practice office.

At work, I never gave anyone a hint that I was unhappy at home. Unfortunately, the more confidence I gained as a health professional, the more insecure Damon became, which gave him further reasons to instigate fights. The beatings and name-calling persisted, but by now, I had learned to live with them. I found my joy in taking care of my patients, and in return, they loved and respected me. My work as a nurse had become my ministry.

One morning, a middle-aged woman came in for an appointment. She was elegant but stern and looked away whenever she spoke.

"How may we help you today?" I asked.

"My husband beat me last night," she said. "I don't plan to press charges, but I want to have my bruises documented, just in case."

From Pain to Purpose

I took a deep breath and put on my professional face. I scribbled something in her chart and left the examining room screaming inside. I knew exactly how she felt. I knew the horror, the wounds, and the depth of her despair. I wanted so much to talk to her as a friend.

The rest of the morning, I couldn't get that woman out of my mind. She looked so well put together. No one would have guessed! I could see myself in her, twenty years into the future.

But what was this thing about "pressing charges," I wondered. Had she implied that her husband was doing something illegal when he beat her? If so, then did this mean that my husband also is doing something illegal when he hits me?

I had lunch with another nurse and casually introduced into the conversation the patient who wanted her bruises documented. My friend shrugged, seeming to think nothing of it. But I had to probe further.

"So, can a wife file charge against her own husband?"

"Of course, she can," my friend answered.

"So, you are saying then that domestic abuse is illegal in this country?" I asked.

I had gone through years of college, including nursing school, and had never heard of such a thing.

Taking a big bite from her sandwich, she said in a slightly sarcastic tone, "In all fifty states, baby!"

The conversation moved on. But for the first time, I felt empowered. I didn't know what I was going to do, but one thing I knew for sure: I didn't want to be middle-aged and still struggling with the same pain.

Not long after this, Damon and I were at a laundromat waiting for the clothes to dry. I walked around the room to pass the time when I noticed on the wall a community bulletin board with business cards pinned to it. Out of boredom, I read each card until I came across one that said, "If you are a victim of domestic abuse, call this number."

I looked at Damon and saw that he was watching me. I was afraid to take the business card, so I paced around the room, and every time I came near the board, I glanced at the phone number until I memorized it. A few days later, when Damon was at work, I called the domestic abuse line.

"What do you consider physical abuse?" I asked the woman who answered the phone.

"Any time your spouse or partner touches you intending to hurt you."

Then she added, "Ma'am, are you abused at home?"

I couldn't bring myself to admit it out loud. When the woman asked the same question again, I hung up the phone. I was abused at home, but I was not strong enough to do anything about it. I didn't know that it takes a woman, on average, between five to seven attempts to leave an abusive relationship before she permanently does so. Then, when she finally leaves, she often risks being seriously hurt or killed by her partner. I was terrified to leave Damon, so I became an even greater expert at masquerading. With each passing day, I pushed the pain deeper into my soul.

If the scriptural adage was true, that "weeping may endure for the night, but joy comes in the morning" (Ps 30:5b NKJV), then my morning had not yet come.

It had been almost seven years since I left Romania, and I was desperately homesick. I missed my family, our traditions, and my people. I was tired of being a foreigner in a foreign land and speaking a foreign language. I was worn out of pretending that I was happy. I was sick of being abused by the one who had vowed to love and cherish me.

But, most of all, I wanted to go home to remind myself that I had once been loved—not perfectly, but loved, nevertheless. I wanted to know once again that I was not alone in this world, and maybe if Damon could see that, then he would stop hurting me as if I belonged to no one. Damon finally agreed to go to Romania.

From Pain to Purpose

When I asked for time off, my office manager insisted that I take a whole month to visit. Damon decided to quit his job as a waiter and then look for another one when we returned.

When we walked off the plane in Timişoara, I knelt and kissed the ground under my feet. I was back in the land of my birth and felt instantly at peace. The Romanian language spoken around me was by far the most melodic tune I had heard in years. The bond I felt with passing strangers was nothing I had experienced among strangers in America. I had forgotten how much it warms the soul to be with one's own kind. Romania was safe, and I was safe, at least for the next four weeks.

The first week we visited relatives and old friends from church. At night my parents and I barely slept. We laughed at silly memories and talked about everything we could think of. My mother baked my favorite cakes, and we feasted every day on traditional Romanian foods.

Timişoara looked quite different from how I had last seen it, seven years before. Free market advertisements proudly replaced the old communist signs and slogans. But the country was as beautiful as I remembered it, and I felt that I belonged there. Even Damon seemed to enjoy himself for the first two weeks. But I could sense that his patience was growing thin.

We traveled an entire week around the country with my sister and brother-in-law, visiting centuries-old castles and monasteries, gazing at the majesty of the Carpathian Mountains and Transylvanian plains, and sinking our feet into babbling brooks along the way. It felt good to belong to a family, a country, and a people in whose veins flowed the same blood as my own. It felt especially good to laugh again—really laugh. But as time was running out, I felt my apprehension starting to rise.

When the dreaded day came to say goodbye to my family, we cried, holding on to each other. But no one knew the secret that lay behind my tears. I was returning not to a free country and a loving home, but to a prison where abuse and sorrow were my daily bread, to a prison darker and crueler than the communists could ever invent.

Prison without Walls

Our layover in Vienna was an overnight stay at the airport. I cried so hard that I made myself sick. I could see that nothing had changed inside Damon. When we arrived home, the abuse started almost immediately, and his words were even more injurious than before.

"You are nothing but a barbarian from a third-world country, coming from a pack of Gypsies," he blasted.

Although I carried the financial burden of the home, he still reminded me that I didn't deserve to live in *his* country and eat *his* food. I lived in a nightmare that started daily at the crack of dawn. And when I thought that things could not get any worse, my already shattered world came crumbling down.

Chapter 12

The Way Out

AMID OUR GREATEST PAIN, we humans have learned to find little joys to help us maintain a shred of sanity. For me, walking around a nearby track was that life-giving joy to which I looked forward at the end of each day.

It was a beautiful spring evening, and the Hale-Bopp comet was still visible in the night sky. We walked together for almost an hour before Damon began to talk about what was obviously on his mind.

"Darlene came to work today with a black eye. Her husband beat her again."

I knew Darlene and her husband. We had dinner at their house once.

Damon seemed so protective of Darlene, which irritated me. I listened for the next half an hour as Damon advocated for Darlene's safety and her right to marital bliss, and I debated whether to say something. The fact that we were in a public place gave me courage.

"What about us?" I asked.

"I don't know what you mean," Damon said, with little conviction in his voice.

The Way Out

Outside the walls of our apartment, I had never mentioned his beatings. My bringing it up took him by surprise. To Damon, so long as I kept the abuse secret, it didn't really happen.

"What about when you hit me? Is that not the same?" I asked.

I could tell by his heavy breathing that he was not pleased with my sudden boldness, and I started to regret that I had opened this can of worms. We walked a few more laps before we decided to leave. In the parking lot, I reached for the car door, only to realize that I was alone. I looked back. Damon was still on the track. It was late, and no one else was there except a random guy doing stretches.

"Are you coming?" I asked.

Damon stared in the direction of the guy stretching.

"Who is that? Do you know him?" I continued.

We walked together toward the car.

"I thought you knew," Damon said.

I stalled, trying to prolong the last few moments of my pretend naivety. I knew what he was going to say, but I asked anyway: "Knew what?"

"That I'm sexually attracted to men. I thought you knew."

In the car, Damon glanced at me a few times as if to read my reaction. My inner response surprised me. I was shocked and relieved at the same time. I was shocked that he had finally admitted it since he often spoke disparagingly of gays. And I was relieved because I knew this could be my "biblically justified" way out of a miserable marriage.

"This is how I am, and you need to accept it. And don't you dare ruin *my* marriage," Damon threatened as we entered the house.

If anyone had ruined this marriage, it was not me. But now, with all cards on the table, Damon wanted to make sure that he still had a firm hand in the marriage and that I planned to keep up his charade.

I stayed up late staring into my cup of milk, trying to sort out my thoughts. It all made sense. Whenever Damon talked about his childhood abuse, he always hinted that it left him confused about his sexuality. For a long time, I wasn't sure what that meant, and I was afraid to ask him. Then, there was his behavior during our honeymoon, his nighttime rages, and the fact that he never showed much interest in me sexually. It all made sense now. Over the years, I hesitated to let my thoughts go in that direction, even after a classmate in nursing school had told me bluntly that my husband was gay just by looking at him. But that night, the big question was, just what was I supposed to do now?

For the next couple of months, neither one of us said much at the dinner table. At night I slept quite comfortably on the seam of the mattress. We no longer argued, and he stopped hitting me, which made me feel much more at ease in the house.

Damon managed a twenty-four-hour restaurant, which meant that he came home at various times during the night and day. He liked the fact that I did not question his coming and going. Then, one evening I asked:

"How is your new job?"

"Fine. I'm working with this guy, Matt, who is having marital problems. We stay late sometimes to talk," he said.

I was setting the table and noticed that Damon was pacing.

"Is everything okay?" I asked.

"I need to go. Matt is spending the night with one of the waitresses from work. I can't let that happen. He is a married man."

Damon dashed out the door, leaving me alone at the table. Around 10 p.m., the phone rang.

"Tell your husband that next time he butts into my personal business, I will call the police."

When Damon got home, I gave him Matt's message and then sat on the couch, waiting for an explanation.

"The truth is, I have deep feelings for Matt, and he keeps rejecting me," Damon said.

I was not sure how I was supposed to respond. I had to stop thinking like a wife for a start.

The Way Out

"So, tonight was just a fit of jealousy, not an attempt to prevent Matt from 'sinning'?" I asked. "Have you thought that Matt is probably straight?"

A few weeks later, Matt was fired from his job, and Damon came home crying like a baby.

"I am in agony. I have to see Matt again," he said.

"Are you in love with Matt?"

"Yes," my husband answered.

Without Matt, Damon was no longer happy at work.

"I'm tired of living in a small town. Let's move somewhere else," he said one day.

I liked my job as a nurse and didn't want to move. Nevertheless, Damon accepted a position in Georgia and had to leave for a three-week training course. He never asked me how I felt about the move. He just assumed that I would follow him.

Damon and I had never been apart in seven years of marriage, and now he was taking off for three weeks. When he picked up his suitcase, I nearly lost it. I grabbed his hand and would not let go of him. Despite the abuse and his recent confession, I couldn't imagine a day without him. My codependency was so severe that I begged him with tears not to leave me by myself. But, when his car departed, an incredible sense of freedom came over me as if massive shackles had fallen off my hands and feet.

The company paid for Damon to come home every weekend, but he never did, except for one weekend which he spent with Matt, as he later admitted. That weekend ended in them punching each other! Damon never told me the reason they fought, but I had a pretty good idea. After his training, he went directly to his new job in Georgia and asked me to start packing the house to move.

With Damon away, I felt safe to reevaluate my life and my future. I was almost twenty-nine years old. I had no children. I could financially support myself, and my abusive husband was openly chasing another man. Could I entertain the possibility of divorce? But what would be the consequences? Would God ever forgive

From Pain to Purpose

me? Would I ever be in ministry? Would a godly man marry a divorcee? What would my parents say? I had so many questions. I needed to talk to someone.

◆◆◆

One evening the phone rang.
"Lumi, this is Marcela."
"Marcela? Where are you?"
"I'm here, in America, in Atlanta."

The sound of Marcela's voice could not have been more unexpected, yet it instantly filled me with joy. Marcela was Nuți's cousin, and we became best friends after Nuți had moved away. We were like sisters and often joked that we were separated at birth. When I left Romania, Marcela was the one I missed the most from our youth group. Over the years we kept in touch by letters, but now she was calling from two hours away!

"When can I see you? I can't believe I'm here," she squealed.

Marcela's husband came to America on a work visa the prior year, and Marcela had just won the visa lottery. We talked for an hour, shouting with excitement that neither of us could hear what the other was saying. We made plans to meet the following weekend, and when I hung up the phone, I felt as if life had returned to my body. Could Marcela be my saving grace? I desperately needed for it to be so.

I drove to Atlanta on a Friday night after work. When Marcela and I saw each other, we danced in circles like two little schoolgirls. She reminded me of a time when I was happy and carefree, which now seemed so long ago.

"Please, stay until Sunday," she pled. "We have so much to talk about."

I had already planned to do so.

The first night we didn't sleep at all. Eight years apart took a lot of catching up. The next day we raided the fridge and spent the

The Way Out

entire day in our pajamas. Speaking Romanian again gave me a great boost of morale.

Around midnight, Marcela's husband fell asleep, but she and I continued to reminisce. The night hours ticked away, and I could feel my exhaustion weakening my defenses.

"Marcela, do you remember the lamppost?"

We both smiled.

"Oh, if that lamppost could only speak!" she said.

One of my best childhood memories was walking home from church with Marcela and talking for hours under the streetlight at the intersection where we usually parted ways. We named that streetlight "stâlpul aducerilor aminte" (the lamppost of remembrances). There, surrounded by the night's chill, we shared our secret hopes about the future. We talked about our boyfriends, dreamed about our weddings and how many kids we wanted, and imagined growing old with the love of our life.

"Lumi, there is something I have to tell you," Marcela said, the smile fading from her face.

"When you broke up with Ștefan, you wounded him. There is something you need to know that he never wanted you to find out. You and Ștefan scored the same on the ACT exam. The decision as to which one of you would receive the scholarship fell to Pastor Petrică, who owed a favor to Ștefan's uncle in Switzerland. Ștefan's uncle called Pastor Petrică to ask him to give the scholarship to Ștefan. When the results came in, Ștefan refused the scholarship. He knew how much you wanted it. That's how you came to America."

Marcela's words hit like a freight train.

I shut my eyes.

"I don't believe it! Why didn't he tell me? Why didn't anybody tell me?"

"Ștefan loved you and wanted you to be happy. He knew that he risked losing you if you left Romania, but he did it anyway."

We sat on the floor, leaning on pillows propped against the wall.

"Damon beats me."

Marcela's eyes widened, then she burst into tears.

"He started beating me the day after our honeymoon. I don't know what to do. I want to divorce him, but what if I will always have a second-rate life because I'm divorced?"

"And what kind of life do you have now?" Marcela asked angrily. "Listen, I know what we learned in church about divorce. But, Lumi, I would not stay with a man who beat me, and you shouldn't either. It's not what you deserve. It's not God's will. And it's not the life you dreamed about at the lamppost."

Marcela's words pierced like an arrow. For seven years, I had been afraid of the word *divorce*. I believed that murder and adultery were far more forgivable by God. To me, divorce was the gravest of all sins and was the death penalty for any future ministry. But that night, Marcela reminded me of who I used to be. Abuse has a way of making you forget. That night, Marcela's words gave me back my power. Seeing myself through her eyes was the push I needed, to do what I should have done long before. I wiped my tears, and for the first time since I married Damon, I felt in charge of my life.

I arrived home to find a message on my answering machine. Damon wanted me to bring him more clothes, along with all the household items I could fit into my car.

The following weekend I loaded my Sunfire and headed south to Georgia. Damon waited for me in the parking lot of his new apartment, smoking a cigarette. He didn't smoke before, and seeing him puff away casually, took me by surprise.

We went to dinner at a small Greek restaurant in town. The owner, having already met Damon, came to our table to introduce himself to me. "Tell your husband to stop smoking so much. It is not good for him," the man said, in a heavy Greek accent. I nodded politely, trying not to give away my own dismay about Damon's new habit.

At dinner, the tension between us felt unbearable. We were two strangers with nothing left in common. Every other word out of Damon's mouth was foul. I didn't recognize him anymore. For

The Way Out

most of the evening, he spoke about his new friends, hinting not so subtly that many of them were gay. Later that day, we went to the new restaurant he was managing. The staff appeared shocked when I introduced myself as Damon's wife.

I woke up early the following day to make the ten-hour trip back home. In the parking lot, Damon leaned on my opened car window. "Please help me. I'm spiraling out of control. I need you." This was the first time in our married life that I heard him say these words. I closed the window and drove away.

Before I married Damon, I had often thought about how blessed I was to have come to faith early in life before committing "big" sins. I was proud of my wholesome past, untouched by life-altering mistakes. But now, alone in the car, I wanted out of my marriage and could not think of a sin that God hated more than the one I was contemplating.

I remembered how some people had warned me against marrying Damon, but I didn't listen. I had many chances to walk away before we got married, but I didn't do it. Damon even broke off our engagement for one day, which I never told anyone. Why was I so stubborn? Could God ever fix the mess I had made of my life?

I could barely see the road ahead of me for tears. For the first time, the filth of my own sinfulness disgusted me. All I could say for the next one hundred miles was, "Grace, grace, God's grace. Grace that is greater than all my sins."

I needed God's grace more than I needed my next breath.

I arrived home exhausted but sure of what I had to do. I phoned Joyce and Jerry, an older couple we knew, and told them that I needed to talk with them. Their house was cozy and welcoming, and I always felt good whenever I was there.

I sat on the couch across from them, and, from my hesitance, they guessed that something big was the matter.

"I'm not moving to Georgia with Damon," I said.

The look on their faces was a mixture of shock and concern.

From Pain to Purpose

"He has been beating me ever since we got married. I was scared to tell anyone."

I wasn't sure how Joyce and Jerry would react, but it didn't matter anymore. I was tired of protecting a lie. I looked down, twirling a piece of string around my finger, waiting for them to say anything. Joyce broke the silence.

"Lumi, even if you shouted profanities at Damon every day for the last seven years, he had no right to hit you." Jerry agreed, and they offered to call their pastor to meet with me.

A few days later, I went to their house where their pastor and his wife waited for me. I felt immediately at a disadvantage when I realized that the pastor and his wife were Tennessee Temple graduates and knew Damon quite well from taking classes together. But I didn't care anymore. I had nothing to lose. I told them about the abuse and Damon's sexual preference for males and that I considered filing for divorce.

Barely waiting for me to finish, the pastor interjected, "You know that God hates divorce. The Bible says that divorce is a sin."

His tone was stern and condescending.

"If you are afraid of Damon, you can temporarily separate, but you have to reconcile. If you divorce, you must remain single for the rest of your life. That's what the Bible says."

I stared at him shocked at the way he delivered "God's will" for me. I knew what the Bible said about such things. I didn't need him to quote it for me.

I felt an urge to scream in his face in a fit of anger, to say: "How dare you speak for God? Have you ever taken one slap in the face for him? I have! Have you ever been in prison for this God whose will you think you represent? I have! Have you ever awaited death because you owned this Bible from which you so smugly quote? Well, I have! I have committed no crime to deserve such harsh punishment. You are nothing but a cold-blooded Pharisee!"

But I didn't say those things. Instead, I turned to his wife for comfort. She embodied everything I wanted out of life—to be a pastor's wife who prayed for hurting people, even if I had nothing to say.

The Way Out

"Do you have anything for me?" I asked her.
She shook her head, never taking her eyes off the floor.
"No."
I went home and threw myself on my knees.
"Father, I love you more than I love my own life. I almost died because I didn't deny knowing you in prison. And if I were to live a thousand lives, I would do it all over again, a thousand times. I would rather die than willingly disobey you, but I can't live like this anymore. Tomorrow I will do something I never thought I would do. Tomorrow I will call a divorce lawyer. Forgive me."

It took more than a year to save enough money for a lawyer. Damon didn't know about my plans and called only once during that time. Sometimes he came to town and entered the apartment when I was not there. He took things and posted notes around the house in an encrypted language like *Veni Vidi Vici* (I came, I saw, I conquered). This scared me, and I asked for the locks to be changed. At night, especially, I watched my back when going to my car and coming into the house. In fear of him, I cried myself to sleep many times.

Divorce was a sin, but to me, it was more than a sin. Divorce was a form of death: the death of a dream of having a happy family, the loss of ten years I could never get back, and the end of my calling to ministry. But it was what I needed to do.

When my lawyer told me that my divorce papers had been served on Damon, I braced myself for a phone call that night.

"I don't know who you are anymore," Damon shouted from the other end of the line. "I'm not signing anything. I threw the papers in the trash. I just wanted you to know."

The fact that Damon didn't know who I was anymore was a good thing. It was proof that I was taking back my power, and it felt amazing. The next day he called my lawyer to request changes to the divorce papers.

From Pain to Purpose

"We represent your wife, not you. We only make changes if your wife requests them. Get your own lawyer," my legal advisor fired back.

Damon was trying to contest the divorce.

"I won't let you destroy my marriage and my reputation," his voice shrieked through the receiver.

He had always referred to our marriage as *his* marriage. I never understood that until then. Just like our house was *his* house and our wedding was *his* wedding, so had our marital union existed only for him, as a cover-up for the life he was living. It didn't even matter that we lived in two different states or had not talked for an entire year, so long as he could say that he was married if anyone suspected that he was gay. He needed me as a wife to make him look respectable, despite the personal cost to me. But I was no longer willing to make that sacrifice.

"Right now, the grounds for divorce are irreconcilable differences," I told Damon. "If you contest the divorce, I will have to change them to 'inappropriate marital conduct.' Let me know what you decide."

My calm infuriated Damon, and when he began to curse, I hung up the phone. I refused to be disrespected anymore.

At the end of that year, I walked alone into an empty courtroom, during my lunch break, and stood before a judge who dissolved our marriage.

It had been ten years since I came to this country, wide-eyed and with big hopes, certain that no one could hurt me here. I was now thirty years old, single, and miles from my childhood dreams that brought me to this land.

Sometimes, late at night, I still thought about ministry. But deep inside, I could not shake the feeling that I was becoming angry with God.

Chapter 13

"Do You Love Me?"

THE PLAYGROUND NEAR MY office became my lunchtime retreat. Children's laughter had a way of helping me forget my troubles, even if only for a moment. After my divorce, some said that I looked solemn. So, I decided to smile more often, especially around children.

"Come on and jump. Daddy will catch you!" a father beckoned to his little girl sitting on the swing next to me.

Her pigtails flung from side to side. Her tiny fingers wrapped tightly around the chain made it clear that she was not about to jump.

"I promise. Daddy will catch you."

She looked into her father's eyes and slowly let go of the chain, one hand at a time. The next moment, she abandoned herself in her father's strong hands. He squeezed her to his chest and threw her up in the air.

"Again," she giggled.

With each jump, the little girl's fingers let go quicker from the security of the chain as she flew into the waiting arms of her father.

I walked to a bench under a tree to be alone.

"Father, I trusted you with the biggest leap of my life, and you dropped me! You knew my heart. I didn't come to America to be rich. Plenty of people do that. All I wanted was to marry a godly man so together we might serve you. Why didn't you stop me from making such an irreparable mistake? How can I trust you again with my next jump?"

My sister and her family had just moved to Australia, where my brother-in-law had accepted a call to pastor a Romanian church. One day my phone rang.

"Hey, this is Dorina. Guess who's at our house? Cristian! Do you want to talk to him?"

Cristian had been married for ten years by then and had five children. He was a pastor and had become a household-name evangelist in Romania. At that time, he was on a month-long speaking tour to Romanian churches throughout Australia.

I congratulated him on his large family and offered my condolences about the passing of his mother. He loved her enormously, and I knew his loss was immense. But Cristian didn't want to talk about that. My sister had told him about my divorce.

"Lumi, I want to ask you only one question. Did you ever love me?"

His question surprised me. I didn't think it mattered anymore. But clearly, it still mattered to him.

"Cristian, you were the only man I ever loved."

I could hear him let out a long, heavy sigh.

"Then why did you break up with me?"

"Because you were so possessive and jealous. You scared me. We argued all the time. Remember?"

"I'm sorry about your divorce. I pray that your third marriage will be better," Christian said.

"Third marriage?" I asked confused.

"Yes! I was supposed to be your husband. That was God's perfect will for us. Your next husband will be your third in God's eyes."

"Do You Love Me?"

"What? What convoluted theology was that?" I thought. While I disagreed, I didn't want to press the point.

"Cristian, can I ask you one question? Why did you marry so quickly after we broke up?"

"The Bible says that it's better to marry than to burn. At that age, I was a burning ball of hormones and I needed to calm them down," he said, chuckling.

We both laughed, and I thought we had reached a good place to end the call. But Cristian wanted to continue. He mostly wanted to compare notes about where he was in life and how I fared ten years after our breakup. I could tell that he felt vindicated. My divorce was clearly my comeuppance for not marrying him.

For the rest of the evening, I cried with loud sobs.

On my thirtieth birthday, I pulled a twelve-hour shift in a nursing home for extra money. No dinners, gifts, or celebrations were planned for me. The drab surroundings of the nursing home summed up perfectly how I felt inside, and the stench of pills and feces accurately described my life. If this was rock bottom, I had reached it!

My nursing assistant, a chubby young man, noticed that I was sad. I told him it was my birthday.

"And you're working? Here?"

He wished me a happy birthday, and during his break, he bought me a card. I had never seen that young man before, nor did I ever see him again. But what I saw in his kindness was a glimpse of God, who maybe hadn't forgotten about me.

After working two jobs during the week and taking shifts in nursing homes on Saturdays, it felt good to be in church again on Sundays. Week after week, I absorbed every word of each sermon, but somehow a twinge of doubt, like a wet blanket, always seemed to stifle the message. Was I becoming jaded about God? What

From Pain to Purpose

happened to the childlike faith I once had that I could walk on water? Was that now a mere theological proposition to which I warily assented?

I oscillated between blaming myself and blaming God for my past. I equally loved him and was angry with him. I knew my worth as God's child, but in my belly, I felt myself to be damaged goods beyond repair. I couldn't stop asking the same two questions over again: Why did I say yes to Damon? And why didn't God stop me from doing so?

I grappled, day and night, with the notion of free will. I wondered why God allows us to make decisions that he knows will hurt us in the end. I wondered why God hadn't stopped Adam and Eve from eating the forbidden fruit when he knew what pain their choice would bring the world.

Could it be that our freedom to make any choices is more important to God than him stopping us from making bad ones? Or is it that we are more useful to God in our brokenness? If so, then the scars we bear are not disfigurements to hide but rather victory badges for the whole world to behold. Perhaps my divorce is not a scarlet letter emblazoned upon my forehead, as something to be ashamed of, but rather a trophy of God's grace inscribed upon my heart with the libretto, "I'm a survivor!"

Whether God had predestined my fall on life's playground, or I leaped at the wrong time of my own free will, I am still here. My pain must have a purpose. It must.

Alone in the house, I spent most of my evenings dwelling upon the past. Then one day I dusted off an old journal I had brought with me from Romania. The pages had turned yellow, and the ink was slightly faded, but the words on the first page grabbed my attention: "To have a weapon against doubt I started this journal today, January 13, 1986."

"A weapon against doubt!" Doubt of what? What did I doubt that required a weapon? The loose pages crackled between my fingers. From a different century and a world that didn't exist

"Do You Love Me?"

anymore, a fifteen-year-old urged me, "Read on and do not doubt, but believe."

Detailed dreams and lavish promises stemming from dozens of hours spent with God leaped off the pages. My calling to ministry—*that* was what I doubted! The journal I held in my hands bore witness that God had spoken to me. It contained proof that he had called me to preach. The promises on each page were the weapon I had long laid down.

I held the journal to my chest. Do I dare believe again?

"Father, I wanted to offer you a perfect life to use, but I couldn't reach that high a pedestal. Could you use a broken vessel instead?" I prayed.

I picked up my Romanian Bible and heard in my spirit: "I called *you* to preach the gospel, not your husband. And I never changed my mind, for my gifts and my call are irrevocable."[1]

I lifted my chin and straightened my shoulders. I was back in the game. But there was one more test I needed to pass.

I took off my wedding band and placed it on a shelf. The indentation it left on my finger betrayed that I had been married a long time.

That evening, I stopped at a gas station before heading to a friend's house.

"Hi," a voice spoke, coming from my left.

One thing I learned from ten years of living in the South was to be nice to everyone. I nodded politely while continuing to watch the numbers on the pump. From the corner of my eye, I saw a man in his late twenties coming closer, smiling.

"I'm sorry to bother you. I was just wondering if you are seeing anyone right now."

"What gall!" I thought.

"Yes! I mean, no! I mean, I'm married," I said, fumbling over my words.

The look on his face said that he didn't believe me.

"But you're not wearing a wedding ring."

"I know. Goodbye."

1. Rom 11:29 KJV.

I jumped into the car and locked the door, my heartbeat pounding in my ears. After ten years, I forgot how to be single again. This was going to be interesting!

For the next several months, I found notes on my windshield from unknown men asking for dates. At traffic lights and in restaurants, someone invariably asked for my phone number. Even some of my patients had noticed my bare finger and asked me out, despite professional boundaries. Where were all these men coming from?

One day, I overheard a nurse in the lunchroom say, "If I looked like Lumi, I would play the field and make men spend money on me. I wouldn't clean butts in a nursing home on weekends."

"She is saving herself for her future husband," another nurse quipped.

I had a pretty good idea of what "playing the field" meant, and it surprised me to hear a Christian nurse saying such a thing. I found a seat at the table and put down my food. Three nurses chimed in, one after another, as if on cue: "Who are you saving yourself for, Lumi? Everybody is playing the field. God will forgive you."

As a teenager, I learned that sexual purity honors both God and my future husband. But now that I was single again and no longer a virgin, I felt tainted. The stigma of a failed marriage followed me like a dark shadow, especially in church circles, and I could not escape it.

Reentering the dating scene after a decade of marriage was daunting. Christian men, in particular, surprised me. Some were no different than unbelievers. They intentionally sought out recently divorced women because they were vulnerable and easily enticed.

Others, who wanted serious relationships, seemed to fall into two categories: those who refused to go out with a divorced woman because she was not a virgin (for the most part, Romanian men fell into that category), and those who dated virtually any woman except a divorcee, for fear of a repeat.

My phone stopped ringing. I was thirty-one years old, single, abstinent, and dateless, wondering if "bringing my body as a living

"Do You Love Me?"

sacrifice to God" was worth the agony of my loneliness. Maybe the nurses were right. Perhaps I had been too self-righteous and "Ms. Goody-Two-Shoes." Maybe there is a "middle-of-the-road."

It was Valentine's Day. The aroma from the oven was mouth-watering. The chocolate-covered strawberries plated perfectly on the doily in front of me, begged to be eaten first. I resisted.

I thought about the glittering gowns and sparkling jewels that were paraded all about town that night. I had never heard of Valentine's Day before I came to America. It didn't hold much meaning to me. Still, I was sad, knowing its significance.

I plated my meal and bowed my head, "Jesus, will you be my Valentine?"

When I finished my dinner, the only dish in the sink reminded me that I was alone, so I left it there. I plopped myself on the couch, with my Bible in my lap, and read the first underlined verse I happened to see.

"God left him, to try him, that he might know all that was in his heart."[2]

Those words immediately snagged my attention. In my spirit, the Lord continued to speak: "I never abandoned you, but I had to know if I could trust you because what I have in store for you will take integrity, obedience, and walking intimately with me."

"Trust me?" I scoffed.

I immediately thought about the man I had dated a few months back. A mutual friend had introduced us, and I agreed to go out with him even though he was not a believer. Within two months, we fell in love, and I was trying to figure out what "the middle of the road" looked like.

Late one evening, after we had finished dinner at my place, I reached slowly for his hand. He pulled me to his chest and whispered: "Stick to your guns, my love. Don't do this for me." I could

---

2. 2 Chr 32:31b KJV.

hear his heartbeat as he spoke. His friends had taunted him because we hadn't slept together, and I knew it bothered him.

He knelt on the floor in front of me.

"Lumi, you're not going to like what I'm about to tell you. You deserve someone who believes like you and will handle you with white gloves for the rest of your life. I am not that man. I'm sorry."

I stared stunned into his green eyes. His words felt like a dagger plunged mercilessly into my heart. But I knew he was right, and I knew it was over. Before he reached for the door, I asked him to hold me one last time. He did, and when he left, he didn't look back.

I ran to the window to watch his truck leave. Tears blurred my vision, and the pain gripped me by the throat, and wouldn't let go. I watched his break lights fade into the distance until they vanished. Then, I toppled onto the living room floor, and for the rest of the evening, I stared motionless at the same spot on the wall.

"Do you love me more than this?" the words of Jesus I had read that morning pressed me for an answer.

The following day I woke up next to a pile of crumpled tissues. I was alone in the world again. I closed my eyes and whispered:

"You know all things, Lord. You know that I love you."

Chapter 14

What Locusts Have Eaten

WHETHER IT WAS SPOKEN or implied, I don't remember, but somehow, I had come to believe that those whom God wants to use, he shelters from making big mistakes in life.

As I think of it, I recall a pastor once saying that the men (!) whom God chooses for ministry are born exclusively into godly families. In that pastor's estimation, the condition for being used mightily by God was to have had a praying mother. That condition never sat well with me. I knew several men and women whom God had used who were first-generation believers.

But the poorest description of God's heart I'd ever heard came from an influential churchwoman who once told me, "You will never be as blessed as my children because God favors the offspring of believers."

I was neither the "son" of a praying mother nor the offspring of believers. So, I grappled with that theology for a long time. Everything I knew of God clashed with it. I couldn't see how a person was more likely to be used by God due sheerly to their family of origin. In the same way, considering the whole counsel of Scripture, I couldn't see how one's call to ministry was strictly dependent upon their gender, or their past being devoid of big mistakes.

From Pain to Purpose

What qualifies me or anyone else in the world to serve God and his church? Is it not plainly and simply God's grace?

As I continued to care for my patients, I could sense my thoughts shifting again toward the ministry. When I dressed their wounds and listened to their hurts, my compassion grew, and I imagined myself doing the same things in remote places of the world. I could feel my joy and my call reawakening within me like a sleeping giant. It has been a long time since my heart leaped for joy about anything. I knew that God had called me to ministry before the divorce, but what did he want of me now?

Every day I rushed home, curled up with my Bible on my favorite corner of the sofa, and waited for God to speak to me. Then, one day I turned to the pages of the book of Revelation.

"Remember then from where you have fallen; repent and do the works you did at first."[1]

The words of the risen Jesus jumped off the page. They sounded firm and straightforward, like a three-step plan for moving on: remember, repent, and do again what you had done before you fell. I knew those words were for me.

For the past two years, I have done nothing but "remember" and "repent." I had wept over my sin of divorce a thousand times. I repented for not having watched and prayed. And I knew exactly why and from where I had fallen. But what was I supposed to do, yet again, that I had done at first? That exhortation was about returning to one's first love, and I knew that my heart had hardened toward God.

Over the years, I had lost my childlike faith. I had become cynical about God's goodness to me. I didn't love him as fiercely and consistently as I once had, and I questioned God's promises much too often. The time had come to return to doing the works I had first done.

---

1. Rev 2:5 KJV.

What Locusts Have Eaten

So, I spent most of my evenings praying for a renewed love for God and faith that could open doors to ministry. A Romanian song became my recurrent prayer at this time:

Nu Te lua după mine, Dumnezeul meu, trage-mă după Tine cât ar fi de greu. Voia Ta, voia Ta. ("Don't mind me and my will, Lord, drag me behind you no matter how much it hurts. Your will, Your will.")

Slowly, my will melted into abandonment at the feet of Jesus. "Even now, Lord, nothing holds me in America. I'm free to go anywhere in the world. I have no more agendas for my life. Your will, or nothing," I prayed.

I surrendered my future to the Lord all over again. And for the first time since the divorce, I felt forgiven and my call to ministry restored. Only one question remained: Where do I go from here?

Owning a personal computer had recently become a trend. So, I bought one with the money I received unexpectedly from a car insurance claim.

I typed the words of my first online search, "How to become a Baptist missionary?" I was determined to find answers. The dial-up screeched painfully until the sluggish pages finally loaded. I read the first line, and my heart sunk.

"A Baptist missionary cannot be divorced." No small print. No exceptions. No grace.

I closed the computer and just wept. I was being punished for a past I couldn't change. I was disqualified from the ministry before a single person knew a single thing about me. The doors were shut. If God wanted to use me, then he would have to pry them open himself.

Going to church was the highlight of my week. I joined the young adult singles class to make friends. Many of them welcomed me into their homes. We went on retreats and ate dinners together after worship and took countless joyrides after church just to talk.

To celebrate my becoming an American citizen, about fifty of them threw a surprise party for me. It was a long-awaited milestone in my life. Gazing around the restaurant, I tried not to cry. I recalled the long years of abuse and isolation that I had endured alone, and now, all these people flooded my life with true friendship. I felt so blessed. Once again, the church had become my family, my joy, my lifeline.

Sometimes, however, when I noticed couples holding hands and laughing, I felt a twinge of pain and wondered if God would ever give me a second chance at marriage. I didn't trust myself, but I wanted it, nevertheless.

At church, my options were slim since most men in our singles class were already "spoken for," or they were unaware that they were! So, I decided to check out a dating website I saw advertised on television.

Eric was an aerospace engineer from Texas, a believer, and four years younger than me. He lived about two hours away in Huntsville, Alabama.

I sent him a quick "hello," and we exchanged brief emails and phone calls, but I remained overly cautious and refused to give him my full name or home address. After a couple of months, we planned our first date. Certain that Eric would be "just another guy," I fell asleep before the date and arrived an hour late. But we hit it off anyway, and from then on, we met in public places nearly every weekend.

Since I didn't know anyone who knew Eric, I asked him for proof that he was who he said he was. It sounded harsh, but he didn't mind it. He took that as an opportunity to be a little "braggy." So, he showed me his 4.0 GPA college diploma, his valedictorian medal as an engineering scholar, and his football playing paraphernalia from high school, and took me to his office where he worked as a missile defense engineer.

What Locusts Have Eaten

I, in turn, told him only the name of the hospital where I worked, enough for Eric to send me flowers there, several times. On Sundays, we went to church together, where I made sure that my friends were the extra pairs of eyes I needed if I were to start a serious relationship again.

Ever since my divorce, holidays have been a lonely time for me. I could hardly wait for them to be over. Every year, I worked on Christmas Day and Thanksgiving and took the night shift on New Year's Eve so the other nurses could be with their families. Many friends and even some patients invited me to their homes for the holidays. I almost always declined. They were family occasions and a stark reminder that I was family to no one. But that year, Eric invited me to go to Texas with him for Thanksgiving. I had always wanted to see real cowboys, ranches, and rodeos. But Eric wanted me to meet his family. We had been dating for only four months. His invitation caught me by surprise.

Eric came from an intact family who loved him and valued being together. In his parents' home, I felt instantly welcomed and accepted. Hearing that I was Romanian, Eric's father surprised me with one of our traditional Romanian dishes, *sarmale*, which he prepared himself. His gesture moved me deeply.

Although I had never been to Dallas, the city's name was familiar to me, as it likely was to nearly everyone in Europe in the 1970s. That was because of the widely popular television series named *Dallas*, which I had seen my parents have a fit over every Saturday night as a small child.

Eric had never heard of the famous TV show, but his parents did, and the following day, they packed the car and surprised me with a trip to Southfork Ranch, where *Dallas* was filmed. I walked the grounds where Bobby, Pamela, and J.R. had walked. I never imagined that I would ever see that place in person in my life. But even more so, I never thought I could be happy again. For the first time in a long time, I felt at home.

Eric's family visited him in Huntsville for Christmas that year, where he and I prepared a feast for them. We ate, talked, and played family games for two days. At one point, during a game, Eric spouted without thinking, "Stop teasing my wife!"

The room went silent.

"I mean, my girlfriend," he immediately corrected himself.

That eliminated any doubt that Eric's parents may have had about things being serious between us. We said goodbye to his family, and I was also ready to go home.

"Stay for a minute. I want to ask you something," Eric said.

He took my hand and led me into his office.

"Lumi, I love you. I want to meet your family. I want to see your country. All you have to do is press 'enter.'"

I looked at the computer screen in front of me, and saw two plane tickets to Romania, waiting to be purchased. I pressed the key and we hugged for a long time. I couldn't believe that I would be on my way to see my family in three months' time.

We flew into Munich and then drove for several hours along the Bavarian Alps to Neuschwanstein Castle. Eric had never seen Europe. The scenery took his breath away. We marveled as we drove down Lovers Lane, linking several picturesque towns and castles in the southern part of Germany.

Surrounded by snowcapped mountains and crystal lakes, Neuschwanstein Castle was a jewel. Built by King Ludwig II of Bavaria, also known as the "Fairytale King," the castle was the inspiration behind Walt Disney's famous princesses' castles. I stared enraptured at the structure towering over me, secretly wishing that this would be the beginning of my own fairytale.

The following day we headed to Venice. Eric and I had committed not to sleep together before marriage, so Eric slept on the floor the entire trip except when the room had two beds.

What Locusts Have Eaten

It was the end of March, and the weather was perfect for a gondola ride on the Grand Canal. Our gondolier's serenade carried us gracefully across the water. There was so much peace and beauty to take in, that I didn't want it to end. As we neared the Rialto Bridge, Eric pulled from his pocket a small box. The gondolier smiled, then looked away.

"Lumi, will you be my wife?"

Eric took my left hand into his and caressed my ring finger.

"If you say 'yes,' I promise to be the best husband, provider, and father that I can be. Will you marry me?"

I looked into the glistening water, soaking in the fullness of that moment.

"Yes, I will."

We reached toward each other to embrace, but our sudden move rocked the gondola, and the gondolier lost his balance. He would have fallen in if it were not for his acrobatic act and the oar that he grasped for dear life. He shouted something in Italian. So much for a romantic moment!

We laughed and gently leaned toward each other to kiss. The gondola glided beneath the Rialto Bridge, and from a certain angle, I could see the moon rays reflecting softly in the perfect facets of my ring.

When we left for Europe, I had a hunch that Eric would ask me to marry him on this trip. But I thought he would do so in Romania in front of my family. Suspecting that this might be the case, Eric wanted to introduce an element of surprise. He changed his plans at the last minute to arrange the gondola ride at dusk for our engagement. I could not have thought of anything more romantic.

We arrived in Timișoara at night. The city appeared cluttered and almost unrecognizable. With no GPS for Romania, I couldn't get my bearings to take us to my parents' house. We drove around the city, hoping that some landmark would spark a shred of memory. Frustrated, Eric stopped the car.

"Lumi, I brought you this far, but I don't know where your parents live. So, you have to remember how to get there."

Later he admitted that for a fleeting moment he thought, "What if she is not really from Romania and had made the whole story up?" If I had only known that, it would have made for a great practical joke!

Above the city skyline, I saw the semi-lit steeple of the cathedral not far away.

"Take me to that cathedral. I know how to get home from there."

We arrived at my parents' apartment late into the night. They waited for us with several courses of food and homemade desserts on the table. Cooking was my mother's favorite way to show love and she was good at it.

After Eric went to sleep, my parents and I talked until the rooster in the neighboring yard began to sing. For thirteen years, they hadn't had the courage to ask what happened to me in prison. They heard of the atrocities that took place there and needed to settle that question. I was surprised that they brought it up, but I could tell that it was important to them.

"To be honest, I never understood it myself. I was the only one in my prison cell who didn't lie about being at the protest and who admitted to being a Christian. Yet, I was the only one who was never interrogated or beaten. No one laid a finger on me."

I could see that my parents felt relieved. That night we also talked about my divorce. It grieved my parents that I had hidden my unhappiness from them.

"You deserve an Oscar for your performance, young lady," my father said only half-jokingly.

"How were you able to hide the abuse so well and for so long while I was there?" he asked.

"I always wanted to show you how much better a Christian marriage was. I was ashamed because I knew it wasn't true. So, I pretended to be happy."

"Sometimes, life deals us a bad hand. It was not your fault," my father comforted me.

"You are neither the first nor the last one to go through this," my mother added.

We spent the rest of the night catching up on the last six years, and I realized that I had forgotten just how hysterically funny my father was.

My sister's move to Australia was hard on my parents. They missed the grandchildren and were very lonely. So, Eric and I decided to spend all our time in Romania with them. We rented a car and asked my parents where in the country they would like to go.

My father longed to visit his birthplace. So, the next day we drove to the village of Domaşnea, where my father was born. He laid flowers at his parents' graves, gently kissing each picture on the tombstones. Then, he gazed into the distance at the rolling hills where, as a boy, before the communists came and took their land, he shepherded his father's flocks. He knew those hills like the back of his hand. But now, they seemed so far and out of reach. I could see my father holding back his tears.

My sister and I had not been very close to my father's side of the family. Looking back, I wish that I had relished more of my father's upbringing and listened with more wonder to the stories of his childhood adventures.

About thirty minutes from the village of Domaşnea is the resort town of Herculane. Legend has it that the Roman god Hercules and members of the Roman aristocracy once bathed in the mineral waters of Herculane. I was eager to show Eric the town.

My mother packed a hefty lunch, and we stopped to eat at a picnic area along the Cerna River. Before we sat to eat, Eric motioned all of us to come closer. He took out a piece of paper and started to read, in Romanian: "Mr. Cristescu, I love your daughter, and I would like to ask for her hand in marriage. I promise to take care of her and make her happy . . ."

It took Eric several minutes to read the entire page while mispronouncing nearly every word. But the more he read, the more my parents and I wiped our tears. Unbeknownst to me, before our trip, Eric had called Marcela and told her what he wanted to say to my father. She translated it into Romanian and helped him with the pronunciation.

My father's response was equally emotional, "I give her to you. Since she left Romania, I never stopped worrying about her. Now, we share that worry. Take care of my girl."

I translated my father's words for Eric, and the men shook hands and kissed on both cheeks. Eric broke open a bottle of champagne that he had hidden inside his jacket the entire day. My mother unveiled a mound of homemade fried chicken and my favorite desserts, and we celebrated Romanian-style by the bank of the river.

Three months later, Eric and I had an intimate wedding ceremony at the Victorian Chapel near Gatlinburg, Tennessee, with only Eric's family and a few close friends in attendance. Marcela was my matron of honor.

We spent our honeymoon in a quiet cabin on top of the Great Smoky Mountains. It was the start of a new life and the peace I needed after the tumultuous decade of the nineties.

Chapter 15

"Feed My Sheep"

ERIC AND I SETTLED into our new townhome on top of Lookout Mountain. Surrounded by the beautiful mountain range, it was the perfect place to start our new life. Eric continued as an aerospace engineer, commuting every day to Huntsville. I worked as a plastic surgery nurse. But my favorite thing was to spend the evenings with Eric, dreaming together about our future. There was something about Eric that put me at ease and freed me to dream. But also, for the first time in my life, I was content with being a wife.

"I wonder how people live in the Northeast," I blurted out one evening at dinner.

"I've thought about the same thing," Eric replied.

For the next few minutes, the conversation picked up momentum. Eric had been considering a new job but didn't want to be the first to mention the idea of moving. If we were to relocate, he wanted me to initiate the conversation.

"How would you like to live in Pennsylvania?" he asked half-jokingly.

Since there was no particular reason for us to stay put, a move was not out of the question. Eric's three-hour daily commute to Huntsville and back was sufficient incentive for us to consider

From Pain to Purpose

making a change. It was not long before Boeing, the world's largest aerospace company, hired Eric as a contract engineer, and I said goodbye to thirteen years of living in the beautiful South.

Pennsylvania was cold in November, so we rushed to buy heavy coats, hats, and boots, which neither of us owned while living in Tennessee.

We settled in a suburb of Philadelphia, and the first thing we did was search online for a Baptist church. When we visited the following Sunday, we were surprised by the warmth these "northerners" showed us.

A group from that church had just returned from a mission trip to Romania and they were excited to share their experience with another Romanian. We talked for a long time after the service ended. We also learned that the congregation was American Baptist, which, to our surprise, was an actual denomination, like the Southern Baptist or General Baptist, although in many respects quite different.

Not long after we joined, the church hosted an event featuring the various ministries it supported. A representative from each ministry reserved a table in the fellowship hall to offer information about their work. One such representative was from Eastern Baptist Theological Seminary.

I stared for several minutes at the large display sign on the wall before I approached the table. I knew the answer to my question, but I wanted to ask anyway.

"Do you admit women to your seminary?" I asked the woman behind the table.

"We do. Sixty percent of our students are women," she said with a big smile.

I was intrigued but not impressed.

"Yes, but do you allow them to study to become pastors, like men?"

I braced myself for the same answer I heard in Bible school. But to my surprise, the woman said, "We make no distinction. Our

"Feed My Sheep"

female students take the same classes as our male students, and many of them go on to be senior pastors of churches."

I looked at her dumbfounded. I never heard anything like that in my life! I knew that women could earn master of divinity degrees. But in most seminaries, women fulfilled different course requirements than their male counterparts, whose courses included homiletics and preaching practicum. I called those women's degrees "pink MDivs," and I was not at all interested.

I asked again to make sure I hadn't misunderstood her.

"So, what you are saying is that women at this seminary study just like men, to become pastors of churches, just like men. Is that correct?"

If not for decorum, I would have grabbed her by the shoulders and shaken her for an answer. My life depended on it.

"Yes. It is," she answered, only half-smiling.

I picked up a brochure and went looking for Eric. How was I going to break it to him that I wanted to go to seminary to become a pastor?

Eric and I adjusted well to our first heavy winter in the Northeast. We now owned shovels, scrapers, rock salt, and chains for the tires, and were ready for the coming years' blizzards. For work, I settled into a part-time position as a nurse in a dermatologist's office.

Our first wedding anniversary was a quiet celebration with just the two of us exchanging gifts and dreaming more about the future.

I had been praying about enrolling in the seminary for several months, and I knew that it was time to talk to Eric about it. I felt guilty for not having shared with him my call to ministry in greater detail, prior to our marriage. Being a pastor's spouse was not an easy task, and I hadn't given him the option to make that decision. But I couldn't wait anymore.

"Honey, there is something I want to talk to you about. It has to do with my career," I said. "You see, when I was fifteen years old, God called me to preach. In Romania and here, people told

141

From Pain to Purpose

me that I couldn't do it because I was a girl. But I found out that American Baptist churches have women pastors. Even our church sponsors a seminary that trains men and women equally for pastoral ministry. It's what I've always wanted to do, I just didn't know that I could."

I waited nervously for Eric's answer. My part-time job as a nurse was mainly to get me out of the house. Since I didn't need to work outside of the home, I could go to school full-time.

"If this is what God called you to do, you must do it, and I will support whatever you decide," Eric said.

His words were music to my ears.

That summer brought a welcome surprise! We found out that we were pregnant with our first baby. To celebrate, Eric planned for us a trip to Paris and London that Christmas. Ever since the day of our marriage, I felt like a princess handled by him with white gloves.

Our baby was born on April 21, and we named her Ana Iova—my grandmother's first and last name, and I instantly loved being a mom.

Eric's career was taking off, and he was considering pursuing a master of business administration degree. We looked at several programs in the United States but ultimately decided on London Business School, an Ivy League MBA program in the United Kingdom, which offered him a scholarship based on his college GPA and near-perfect GMAT score. That same year, I was also accepted into the master of divinity program at Eastern Baptist Theological Seminary, but I deferred my admission until our return to the United States.

We sold both our cars, stored what we owned into PODS, and moved across the ocean to England. For the following three years we traveled to almost every country in Europe and visited my parents several times. I also enrolled in the London School of Theology and took several courses that later transferred to Eastern Seminary.

"Feed My Sheep"

Over the years, I had lost contact with Pastor Petrică Dugulescu, although I had remained friends with his daughters, who visited us several times in London. The truth was, I avoided him. I was ashamed of my divorce and having achieved nothing after he had put his reputation on the line for me.

For many years, he took a lot of flak from other pastors in Romania for having sent the twenty-three of us to America. Pastor Petrică's plan was for us to be educated in various fields and then return home to help rebuild our country. Almost no one returned, and most of us were not even in ministry. The experiment was an epic failure.

I wanted to tell Pastor Petrică that I was going to seminary and planned to enter the ministry. I wanted him to be proud of me. But I didn't think it mattered anymore, so many years later. His daughters insisted that he would love to see me, so we made plans to have dinner at their house the next time we were in Romania. But two months later, after a massive heart attack on January 3, 2008, Pastor Petrică, only in his early sixties, went home to be with the Lord. I never told him how much he meant to me. He brought me to the faith, gave me a future, and was my greatest mentor. But he didn't know it—something I would have to live with.

On July 4, 2008, Eric graduated from London Business School and was recruited by McKinsey, the global management consulting firm. A year later, he transferred from the London office to McKinsey-Philadelphia in the United States, and I began my seminary studies.

We bought our first home, and Teodora, our second daughter, was born. With Eric's help and the help of a great babysitter from a Romanian church, I eventually completed my seminary degree—six years later! Our home church licensed me to preach, and I started travel supplying American Baptist pulpits.

From Pain to Purpose

After graduating with my master of divinity, I worked with the American Baptist Credentialing Committee and received my recommendation to be ordained. For my ordination examination defense, several dozen pastors and laypeople from the area came to support me and ask questions. For the first time in my life, I had to publicly articulate my biblical position on the most controversial issues of the day. Not everyone agreed with my answers, but when I returned to the room for "the decision," the people greeted me with applause and a standing ovation, unanimously approving me for ordination.

That night I couldn't sleep. Every step of my journey, every person, every promise, and every pain that helped me inch my way to this day, came into focus. I was grateful for those who made it easy for me and grateful for those who made it hard to reach this milestone. I could not have done it without either of them. That night, I couldn't help wondering if this was the day God had foreseen when he first called me to ministry as a teenager, and I shuddered to think that I could have so easily missed it.

For my ordination service, I invited my church history professor from seminary, Dr. George Hancock-Stefan, a fellow Romanian, to be the keynote speaker.

During my seminary years, we often spoke about the revolution, and he cried no matter how many times he heard my story. Whenever we met in the hallways at school, we instinctively spoke Romanian, probably because speaking our common language soothed our longing for our beloved country.

But my favorite thing was when, in the middle of his lectures, Dr. Hancock-Stefan would throw in a few Romanian words just for me, and without skipping a beat, he continued lecturing in English, while my classmates looked around the room confused, wondering if they had missed something.

Dr. Hancock-Stefan was the first person who asked me to share my testimony publicly, first in one of his classes, in an amphitheater full of students, and then at his church, where he

"Feed My Sheep"

pastored. He was the perfect choice to speak on my big day. However, neither I nor the audience expected to hear what the good professor said that morning:

> From the moment that I received your invitation, two images kept moving in my head. One is a famous painting by Constantin Daniel Rosenthal entitled "România Revoluționară," painted during the great Romanian revolution of the nineteenth century. Rosenthal participated in that revolution, and you participated in the great revolution of the twentieth century. Like Rosenthal, you have experienced the Romanian jails. Out of those experiences, Rosenthal painted that famous painting which became the symbol of the Romanian people looking for the days when we would be a free nation. Out of your jail experience, you have become a fearless person in the service of the Lord Jesus Christ, and your testimony has stirred the hearts of many people to become more committed to the Lord Jesus Christ.
>
> This week, I called the Dean of the Baptist Seminary in Bucharest to verify that we are participating in a historic event today. As far as we have been able to discern, our Luminitza is the first Romanian Baptist woman to be ordained in the world. Neither the Romanian Baptist Convention of Romania nor the Romanian Baptist Association of USA and Canada, have ever ordained a woman. That honor goes to American Baptist Churches USA and the Baptist Church of West Chester who today are ordaining the first Romanian Baptist woman.[1]

The volcanic applause lasted several minutes. People throughout the sanctuary stood, shouted, and whistled. All I could do was weep. It was the culmination of a life's dream unfolding before me. A combination of a stubborn refusal to give up and the faithfulness of a God who cannot lie. That day, I became a Reverend, a title that still startles me when I hear it next to my name. A few months later, I accepted the call to my first pastorate as their first female pastor, a ministry that has been both challenging and rewarding.

1. https://www.abc-usa.org/2016/09/nichols-shares-the-joy-of-american-baptist-ordination/.

From Pain to Purpose

Today, as I live out my purpose in the world, my grandmother's words still echo in my ears, and have become my charge to the churches:

"Keep the faith until the end."

Nuți and me before baptism in the courtyard of the
church, March 18, 1984 (me—at the right)

My church—Bethany Baptist Church (Biserica
Baptistă Betania—Timișoara) ca. 1980s

The revolution, December 1989

My baptism, March 18, 1984 (me—second front
row from the left; Nuți is to my left)

The revolution—people kneeling in the Square when Pastor Petrică led them into the Lord's Prayer. December 1989

April 1986—my sister Dorina's baptism (front row on the left—Pastor Petrică Dugulescu. Top row from the left—my sister Dorina, and to her left is Marcela)

My grandmother, Măicuța (in the middle)—next to her is her mother and my grandfather. They started the first Baptist church in their village of Râpa in the late 1920s (picture taken ca. 1950s)

Lumi preaching at the first church she pastored—2017

Lumi's ordination—2016

www.ingramcontent.com/pod-product-compliance
Lightning Source LLC
Chambersburg PA
CBHW050821160426
43192CB00010B/1849